Taste of Home
ONE-DISH
RECIPES

TASTE OF HOME BOOKS • RDA ENTHUSIAST BRANDS, LLC • MILWAUKEE, WI

© 2019 RDA Enthusiast Brands, LLC.
1610 N. 2nd St., Suite 102, Milwaukee WI 53212-3906

All rights reserved. Taste of Home is a registered trademark of RDA Enthusiast Brands, LLC.

Visit **tasteofhome.com** for other Taste of Home books and products.

International Standard Book Number:
978-1-61765-887-7
Library of Congress Control Number: 2019934844
Component Number: 118600021H

Deputy Editor: Mark Hagen
Senior Art Director: Raeann Thompson
Editor: Hazel Wheaton
Art Director: Maggie Conners
Designer: Arielle Jardine
Copy Editor: Amy Rabideau Silvers

Cover
Photographer: Dan Roberts
Set Stylist: Stacey Genaw
Food Stylist: Shannon Norris

Pictured on front cover:
One-Pot Bacon Cheeseburger Pasta, p. 242
Pictured on title page:
Creamy Spinach & Rigatoni Bake, p. 210
Pictured on back cover:
Lemon-Dijon Pork Sheet-Pan Supper, p. 11
Three-Cheese Meatball Mostaccioli, p. 229
Easy Chicken & Dumplings, p. 98
Pictured on spine:
Tomato Baguette Pizza, p. 241

Printed in China
1 3 5 7 9 10 8 6 4 2

LIKE US
facebook.com/tasteofhome

TWEET US
twitter.com/tasteofhome

FOLLOW US
@ tasteofhome

PIN US
pinterest.com/taste_of_home

SHOP WITH US shoptasteofhome.com   **SHARE A RECIPE** tasteofhome.com/submit

134

126

85

218

153

CONTENTS

Sheet Pan 6

Skillet 38

Dutch Oven 80

Slow Cooker & Instant Pot 124

Casseroles 166

Pizzas & Pastas 208

Index 254

THE ONLY THING EASIER THAN THE RECIPES IS THE CLEANUP!

20

129

Oven-roasted or simmered on the stovetop, simplicity is key when you're getting dinner on the table. And what could be simpler than a self-contained meal-in-one dish?

One-dish meals are more popular than ever—and this new volume collects 118 great recipes that deliver all-in-one convenience perfect for today's busy schedules. Home cooks across the country have shared their favorite recipes with us, and now we're sharing them with you.

From stir-fries and skillet suppers that come together quickly on the stovetop to complete oven-roasted sheet-pan dinners, these recipes offer the ultimate in efficiency. Pastas and pizzas make crowd-pleasing meals that will have even the pickiest eaters asking for seconds. Satisfying casseroles and hearty Dutch oven creations are just right for family dinners all through the week. And for home cooks who love ultra-convenient kitchen gadgets, a chapter features tasty slow-cooker and Instant Pot® recipes.

250

No matter what cookware you use, the recipes in *Taste of Home One-Dish Recipes* help you work your magic in the kitchen any night of the week. The first payoff is when your family savors the meal you've made; the second is when it's time for cleanup. Choose a recipe, choose a dish, and get started cooking today!

246

217

All our recipes are approved by the **Taste of Home Test Kitchen**, so you know every one will turn out just right. Full-color photos with each recipe show you the way, and the easy-to-read large-print format guarantees you'll never have to struggle to read the instructions or measurements.

**TURKEY-STUFFED
BELL PEPPERS, 23**

CHAPTER 1

SHEET PAN

A perfectly self-contained meal all in one pan—
the only thing easier than the recipe is the cleanup!

Curry-Roasted Turkey & Potatoes. 8

Lemon-Dijon Pork Sheet-Pan Supper 11

Sweet & Tangy Salmon with Green Beans. 12

Turkey Lattice Pie. 15

Parmesan Chicken with Artichoke Hearts 16

Pork & Asparagus Sheet-Pan Dinner 19

Spicy Roasted Sausage, Potatoes & Peppers 20

Turkey-Stuffed Bell Peppers 23

Mediterranean Tilapia. 24

Balsamic Roasted Chicken Thighs with Root Vegetables. 27

Roasted Curried Chickpeas & Cauliflower 28

Caesar Salmon with Roasted Tomatoes & Artichokes 31

Pan-Roasted Chicken & Vegetables. 32

Cod & Asparagus Bake 35

Orange-Glazed Pork with Sweet Potatoes 36

CURRY-ROASTED TURKEY & POTATOES

Honey mustard is the go-to condiment around here, so I wanted a healthy recipe to serve it with. Roasted turkey with a dash of curry fits the bill!
—Carol Wit, Tinley Park, IL

. . . .

TAKES: 30 min. • **MAKES:** 4 servings

1 lb. Yukon Gold potatoes (about 3 medium), cut into ½-in. cubes
2 medium leeks (white portion only), thinly sliced
2 Tbsp. canola oil, divided
½ tsp. pepper, divided
¼ tsp. salt, divided
3 Tbsp. Dijon mustard
3 Tbsp. honey
¾ tsp. curry powder
1 pkg. (17.6 oz.) turkey breast cutlets
Minced fresh cilantro or thinly sliced green onions, optional

1. Preheat oven to 450°. Place potatoes and leeks in a 15x10x1-in. baking pan coated with cooking spray. Drizzle with 1 Tbsp. oil; sprinkle with ¼ tsp. pepper and ⅛ tsp. salt. Stir to coat. Roast 15 minutes, stirring once.

2. Meanwhile, in a small bowl, combine mustard, honey, curry powder and the remaining oil. Sprinkle turkey with the remaining salt and pepper.

3. Drizzle 2 Tbsp. of the mustard mixture over the potatoes; stir to coat. Place turkey over the potato mixture; drizzle with the remaining mustard mixture. Roast 6-8 minutes longer or until the turkey is no longer pink and the potatoes are tender. If desired, sprinkle with cilantro.

3 OZ. COOKED TURKEY WITH ¾ CUP POTATO MIXTURE: 393 cal., 9g fat (1g sat. fat), 71mg chol., 582mg sod., 44g carb. (16g sugars, 3g fiber), 33g pro. *Diabetic exchanges:* 4 lean meat, 3 starch, 1½ fat.

LEMON-DIJON PORK SHEET-PAN SUPPER

Most nights, I need something on the table with minimal effort and maximum results. This sheet-pan supper has become an all-time favorite, not only because of its bright flavors, but also because of its speedy cleanup time!
—*Elisabeth Larsen, Pleasant Grove, UT*

PREP: 20 min. • **BAKE:** 20 min. • **MAKES:** 4 servings

4 tsp. Dijon mustard
2 tsp. grated lemon zest
1 garlic clove, minced
½ tsp. salt
2 Tbsp. canola oil
1½ lbs. sweet potatoes (about 3 medium), cut into ½-in. cubes
1 lb. fresh Brussels sprouts (about 4 cups), quartered
4 boneless pork loin chops (6 oz. each)
Coarsely ground pepper, optional

1. Preheat oven to 425°. In a large bowl, mix the first 4 ingredients; gradually whisk in oil. Remove 1 Tbsp. of the mixture for brushing pork. Add the vegetables to the remaining mixture; toss to coat.

2. Place pork chops and vegetables in a 15x10x1-in. pan coated with cooking spray. Brush chops with the reserved mustard mixture. Roast 10 minutes.

3. Turn chops and stir vegetables; roast until a thermometer inserted in the pork reads 145° and vegetables are tender, 10-15 minutes. If desired, sprinkle with coarsely ground pepper. Let stand 5 minutes before serving.

1 PORK CHOP WITH 1¼ CUPS VEGETABLES: 516 cal., 17g fat (4g sat. fat), 82mg chol., 505mg sod., 51g carb. (19g sugars, 9g fiber), 39g pro. *Diabetic exchanges:* 5 lean meat, 3 starch, 1½ fat, 1 vegetable.

SWEET & TANGY SALMON WITH GREEN BEANS

I'm always up for new ways to cook salmon. In this dish, a sweet sauce gives the fish and green beans some down-home barbecue tang. Even our kids love it.
—*Aliesha Caldwell, Robersonville, NC*

PREP: 20 min. • **BAKE:** 15 min. • **MAKES:** 4 servings

4 salmon fillets (6 oz. each)
1 Tbsp. butter
2 Tbsp. brown sugar
2 Tbsp. reduced-sodium soy sauce
2 Tbsp. Dijon mustard
1 Tbsp. olive oil
½ tsp. pepper
⅛ tsp. salt
1 lb. fresh green beans, trimmed

1. Preheat oven to 425°. Place salmon fillets in a 15x10x1-in. baking pan coated with cooking spray. In a small skillet, melt butter; stir in brown sugar, soy sauce, mustard, oil, pepper and salt. Brush half of the mixture over the salmon.

2. Place green beans in a large bowl; drizzle with the remaining brown sugar mixture and toss to coat. Arrange green beans around the fillets. Roast until fish just begins to flake easily with a fork and green beans are crisp-tender, 14-16 minutes.

1 FILLET WITH ¾ CUP GREEN BEANS: 394 cal., 22g fat (5g sat. fat), 93mg chol., 661mg sod., 17g carb. (10g sugars, 4g fiber), 31g pro. *Diabetic exchanges:* 5 lean meat, 1½ fat, 1 vegetable, ½ starch.

TURKEY LATTICE PIE

With its pretty lattice crust, this cheesy baked dish is as appealing as it is tasty. It's easy to make, too, since it uses ready-to-go crescent roll dough.
—*Lorraine Naig, Emmetsburg, IA*

PREP: 20 min. • **BAKE:** 20 min. • **MAKES:** 12 servings

3 tubes (8 oz. each) refrigerated crescent rolls
4 cups cubed cooked turkey
1½ cups shredded cheddar or Swiss cheese
3 cups frozen chopped broccoli, thawed and drained
1 can (10¾ oz.) condensed cream of chicken soup, undiluted
1⅓ cups whole milk
2 Tbsp. Dijon mustard
1 Tbsp. dried minced onion
½ tsp. salt
  Dash pepper
1 large egg, lightly beaten

1. Preheat oven to 375°. Unroll 2 tubes of crescent roll dough; separate into rectangles. Place rectangles in an ungreased 15x10x1-in. baking pan. Press onto the bottom and ¼ in. up the sides of pan to form a crust, sealing the seams and perforations. Bake for 5-7 minutes or until light golden brown.

2. In a large bowl, combine turkey, cheese, broccoli, soup, milk, mustard, onion, salt and pepper. Spoon over crust.

3. Unroll remaining dough; divide into rectangles. Seal perforations. Cut each rectangle into four 1-in. strips. Using strips, make a lattice design on top of turkey mixture. Brush with egg. Bake 17-22 minutes longer or until top crust is golden brown and filling is bubbly.

1 PIECE: 396 cal., 20g fat (4g sat. fat), 81mg chol., 934mg sod., 30g carb. (8g sugars, 2g fiber), 24g pro.

PARMESAN CHICKEN WITH ARTICHOKE HEARTS

I've loved the combo of chicken and artichoke for a long time.
Here's my own lemony twist. With all the praise it gets,
this dinner is so much fun to serve.
—*Carly Giles, Hoquiam, WA*

PREP: 20 min. • **BAKE:** 20 min. • **MAKES:** 4 servings

4 boneless skinless
   chicken breast halves
   (6 oz. each)
3 tsp. olive oil, divided
1 tsp. dried rosemary,
   crushed
½ tsp. dried thyme
½ tsp. pepper
2 cans (14 oz. each)
   water-packed artichoke
   hearts, drained
   and quartered
1 medium onion,
   coarsely chopped
½ cup white wine or
   reduced-sodium
   chicken broth
2 garlic cloves, chopped
¼ cup shredded
   Parmesan cheese
1 lemon, cut into 8 slices
2 green onions,
   thinly sliced

1. Preheat oven to 375°. Place chicken in a 15x10x1-in. baking pan coated with cooking spray; drizzle with 1½ tsp. oil. In a small bowl, mix rosemary, thyme and pepper; sprinkle half of the herb mixture over chicken.

2. In a large bowl, combine artichoke hearts, onion, wine, garlic, the remaining oil and the remaining herb mixture; toss to coat. Arrange around chicken. Sprinkle the chicken with cheese; top with lemon slices.

3. Roast until a thermometer inserted in chicken reads 165°, 20-25 minutes. Sprinkle with green onions.

1 CHICKEN BREAST HALF WITH ¾ CUP ARTICHOKE MIXTURE: 339 cal., 9g fat (3g sat. fat), 98mg chol., 667mg sod., 18g carb. (2g sugars, 1g fiber), 42g pro. *Diabetic exchanges:* 5 lean meat, 1 vegetable, 1 fat, ½ starch.

PORK & ASPARAGUS SHEET-PAN DINNER

When time is of the essence, it's nice to have a quick and easy meal idea in your back pocket. Not only is this sheet-pan meal delicious, but you can clean it up in a flash.
—*Joan Hallford, North Richland Hills, TX*

PREP: 20 min. • **BAKE:** 20 min. • **MAKES:** 4 servings

¼ cup olive oil, divided
3 cups diced new potatoes
3 cups cut fresh asparagus (1-in. pieces)
¼ tsp. salt
¼ tsp. pepper
1 large gala or Honeycrisp apple, peeled and cut into ½-in. slices
2 tsp. brown sugar
1 tsp. ground cinnamon
¼ tsp. ground ginger
4 boneless pork loin chops (1 in. thick and about 6 oz. each)
2 tsp. southwest seasoning

1. Preheat oven to 425°. Line a 15x10x1-in. baking pan with foil; brush with 2 tsp. olive oil.

2. In a large bowl, toss potatoes with 1 Tbsp. olive oil. Place in 1 section of the prepared baking pan. In the same bowl, toss asparagus with 1 Tbsp. olive oil; place in another section of the pan. Sprinkle salt and pepper over potatoes and asparagus.

3. In same bowl, toss apple with 1 tsp. olive oil. In a small bowl, mix brown sugar, cinnamon and ginger; sprinkle over the apples and toss to coat. Transfer to a different section of the pan.

4. Brush pork chops with the remaining olive oil; sprinkle both sides with southwest seasoning. Place chops in the remaining section of the pan. Bake until a thermometer inserted in pork reads 145° and the potatoes and apples are tender, 20-25 minutes. Let stand 5 minutes before serving.

1 SERVING: 486 cal., 23g fat (5g sat. fat), 82mg chol., 447mg sod., 32g carb. (10g sugars, 5g fiber), 37g pro.

SPICY ROASTED SAUSAGE, POTATOES & PEPPERS

I love to share my cooking, and this hearty meal-in-one has gotten a savory reputation around town. People have actually approached me in public to ask for the recipe.
—*Laurie Sledge, Brandon, MS*

PREP: 20 min. • **BAKE:** 30 min. • **MAKES:** 4 servings

1 lb. potatoes (about 2 medium), peeled and cut into ½-in. cubes
1 pkg. (12 oz.) fully cooked andouille chicken sausage links or flavor of your choice, cut into 1-in. pieces
1 medium red onion, cut into wedges
1 medium sweet red pepper, cut into 1-in. pieces
1 medium green pepper, cut into 1-in. pieces
½ cup pickled pepper rings
1 Tbsp. olive oil
½ to 1 tsp. Creole seasoning
¼ tsp. pepper

1. Preheat oven to 400°. In a large bowl, combine potatoes, sausage, onion, red pepper, green pepper and pepper rings. Mix the olive oil, Creole seasoning and pepper; drizzle over the potato mixture and toss to coat.

2. Transfer to a 15x10x1-in. baking pan coated with cooking spray. Roast until the vegetables are tender, stirring occasionally, 30-35 minutes.

1½ CUPS: 257 cal., 11g fat (3g sat. fat), 65mg chol., 759mg sod., 24g carb. (5g sugars, 3g fiber), 17g pro. *Diabetic exchanges:* 3 lean meat, 1 starch, 1 vegetable, 1 fat.

TURKEY-STUFFED BELL PEPPERS

This well-seasoned entree is so tasty, you won't even miss having real cheddar cheese. Round out the meal with a salad or a side of rice.
—*Judy Hand-Truitt, Birmingham, AL*

PREP: 30 min. • **BAKE:** 20 min. • **MAKES:** 5 servings

5 medium green, red or yellow peppers
2 tsp. olive oil
1¼ lbs. extra-lean ground turkey
1 large onion, chopped
1 garlic clove, minced
2 tsp. ground cumin
1 tsp. Italian seasoning
½ tsp. salt
½ tsp. pepper
2 medium tomatoes, finely chopped
1¾ cups shredded cheddar-flavored lactose-free or other cheese
1½ cups soft bread crumbs
¼ tsp. paprika

1. Preheat oven to 325°. Cut peppers lengthwise in half; remove seeds. Place in a 15x10x1-in. pan coated with cooking spray.

2. In a large skillet, heat oil over medium-high heat. Cook and crumble turkey with onion, garlic and seasonings over medium-high heat until the meat is no longer pink, 6-8 minutes. Cool slightly. Stir in tomatoes, cheese and bread crumbs.

3. Fill peppers with turkey mixture. Sprinkle with paprika. Bake, uncovered, until heated through and peppers are tender, 20-25 minutes.

NOTE: Some breads/bread crumbs are made with milk. If you need to be sure your recipe is lactose-free, read the label or ask your baker.

2 STUFFED PEPPER HALVES: 323 cal., 10g fat (0 sat. fat), 45mg chol., 771mg sod., 20g carb. (6g sugars, 4g fiber), 40g pro. *Diabetic exchanges:* 5 lean meat, 2 vegetable, 1 starch, ½ fat.

MEDITERRANEAN TILAPIA

I recently became a fan of tilapia. Its mild taste makes it easy to top with my favorite ingredients. Plus, it's low in calories and fat. What's not to love?
—*Robin Brenneman, Hilliard, OH*

TAKES: 20 min. • **MAKES:** 6 servings

6 tilapia fillets (6 oz. each)
1 cup canned Italian diced tomatoes
½ cup water-packed artichoke hearts, chopped
½ cup sliced ripe olives
½ cup crumbled feta cheese

Preheat oven to 400°. Place fillets in a 15x10x1-in. baking pan coated with cooking spray. Top with tomatoes, artichoke hearts, olives and cheese. Bake, uncovered, until the fish flakes easily with a fork, 15-20 minutes.

1 FILLET: 197 cal., 4g fat (2g sat. fat), 88mg chol., 446mg sod., 5g carb. (2g sugars, 1g fiber), 34g pro. *Diabetic exchanges:* 5 lean meat, ½ fat.

ITALIAN TILAPIA: Follow method as directed but top fillets with 1 cup diced tomatoes with roasted garlic, ½ cup each julienned roasted sweet red pepper, sliced fresh mushrooms, diced fresh mozzarella cheese and ½ tsp. dried basil.

1 FILLET: 189 cal., 4 g fat (2 g sat. fat), 90 mg chol., 351 mg sod., 4 g carb., trace fiber, 34 g pro. *Diabetic exchanges:* 5 lean meat, ½ fat.

SOUTHWEST TILAPIA: Follow method as directed but top fillets with 1 cup diced tomatoes with mild green chiles, ½ each cup cubed avocado, thawed corn, cubed cheddar cheese and ½ tsp. dried cilantro.

1 FILLET: 224 cal., 7 g fat (3 g sat. fat), 93 mg chol., 281 mg sod., 7 g carb., 2 g fiber, 35 g pro. *Diabetic exchanges:* 5 lean meat, 1 fat.

BALSAMIC ROASTED CHICKEN THIGHS WITH ROOT VEGETABLES

I will always remember the way my grandmother's house smelled
when she made this chicken every Sunday. Ever since she gave me the recipe,
the heartwarming flavors always take me back to my childhood.
—*Erin Chilcoat, Central Islip, NY*

PREP: 15 min. + marinating • **BAKE:** 35 min. • **MAKES:** 6 servings

4 Tbsp. olive oil, divided
3 Tbsp. stone-ground
   mustard
2 Tbsp. balsamic
   vinaigrette
¾ tsp. kosher salt, divided
¾ tsp. freshly ground
   pepper, divided
6 bone-in chicken thighs
   (about 2¼ lbs.)
4 medium parsnips,
   peeled and cut into
   ½-in. pieces
1 medium sweet potato,
   peeled and cut into
   ½-in. pieces
4 shallots, chopped
¼ tsp. caraway seeds
4 Tbsp. minced fresh
   parsley, divided
3 bacon strips, cooked
   and crumbled, divided

1. In a bowl, whisk 3 Tbsp. oil, the mustard, vinaigrette and ½ tsp. each salt and pepper until blended. Add chicken, turning to coat. Refrigerate, covered, 6 hours or overnight.

2. Preheat oven to 425°. Place chicken, skin side up, on half of a greased 15x10x1-in. baking pan. Place parsnips and sweet potato in a large bowl. Add the shallots, caraway seeds and remaining oil, salt and pepper; toss to combine. Arrange in a single layer on the remaining half of pan.

3. Roast chicken and vegetables for 20 minutes. Stir vegetables; continue roasting 15-20 minutes longer or until a thermometer inserted in chicken reads 170°-175° and vegetables are tender.

4. Transfer vegetables to a bowl; toss with 2 Tbsp. parsley and half of the bacon. Serve chicken with vegetables; sprinkle chicken with the remaining parsley and bacon.

1 SERVING: 480 cal., 27g fat (6g sat. fat), 85mg chol., 604mg sod., 33g carb. (10g sugars, 5g fiber), 27g pro.

ROASTED CURRIED CHICKPEAS & CAULIFLOWER

When there's not much time to cook, try roasting potatoes and cauliflower with chickpeas for a warm-you-up dinner. It's a filling meal on its own, but you can also add chicken or tofu to the sheet pan if you like.

—*Pam Correll, Brockport, PA*

PREP: 15 min. • **BAKE:** 30 min. • **MAKES:** 4 servings

2 lbs. potatoes (about 4 medium), peeled and cut into ½-in. cubes
1 small head cauliflower, broken into florets (about 3 cups)
1 can (15 oz.) chickpeas, rinsed and drained
3 Tbsp. olive oil
2 tsp. curry powder
¾ tsp. salt
¼ tsp. pepper
3 Tbsp. minced fresh cilantro or parsley

1. Preheat oven to 400°. Place the first 7 ingredients in a large bowl; toss to coat. Transfer to a 15x10x1-in. baking pan coated with cooking spray.

2. Roast until vegetables are tender, 30-35 minutes, stirring occasionally. Sprinkle with cilantro.

1½ CUPS: 339 cal., 13g fat (2g sat. fat), 0 chol., 605mg sod., 51g carb. (6g sugars, 8g fiber), 8g pro. *Diabetic exchanges:* 3 starch, 2 fat, 1 vegetable, 1 lean meat.

CAESAR SALMON WITH ROASTED TOMATOES & ARTICHOKES

This is my go-to recipe for quick dinners for family or guests. This dish is colorful, healthy, easy to prepare and absolutely delicious. Hard to believe it takes only five ingredients!
—*Mary Hawkes, Prescott, AZ*

TAKES: 25 min. • **MAKES:** 4 servings

4 salmon fillets (5 oz. each)
5 Tbsp. reduced-fat Caesar vinaigrette, divided
¼ tsp. pepper, divided
2 cups grape tomatoes
1 can (14 oz.) water-packed artichoke hearts, drained and quartered
1 medium sweet orange or yellow pepper, cut into 1-in. pieces

1. Preheat oven to 425°. Place salmon on half of a 15x10x1-in. baking pan coated with cooking spray. Brush with 2 Tbsp. vinaigrette; sprinkle with ⅛ tsp. pepper.

2. In a large bowl, combine tomatoes, artichoke hearts and sweet pepper. Add the remaining vinaigrette and pepper; toss to coat. Place the tomato mixture on the remaining half of pan. Roast until fish just begins to flake easily with a fork and the vegetables are tender, 12-15 minutes.

1 FILLET WITH ¾ CUP TOMATO MIXTURE: 318 cal., 16g fat (3g sat. fat), 73mg chol., 674mg sod., 12g carb. (4g sugars, 2g fiber), 28g pro. *Diabetic exchanges:* 4 lean meat, 1 vegetable, 1 fat.

PAN-ROASTED CHICKEN & VEGETABLES

This meal tastes as if it took hours of hands-on time, but the simple ingredients can be prepped in minutes. The rosemary gives it a rich flavor, and the meat juices cook the veggies to perfection. So easy!
—*Sherri Melotik, Oak Creek, WI*

PREP: 15 min. • **BAKE:** 45 min. • **MAKES:** 6 servings

2 lbs. red potatoes (about 6 medium), cut into ¾-in. pieces
1 large onion, coarsely chopped
2 Tbsp. olive oil
3 garlic cloves, minced
1¼ tsp. salt, divided
1 tsp. dried rosemary, crushed, divided
¾ tsp. pepper, divided
½ tsp. paprika
6 bone-in chicken thighs (about 2¼ lbs.), skin removed
6 cups fresh baby spinach (about 6 oz.)

1. Preheat oven to 425°. In a large bowl, combine the potatoes, onion, oil, garlic, ¾ tsp. salt, ½ tsp. rosemary and ½ tsp. pepper; toss to coat. Transfer to a 15x10x1-in. baking pan coated with cooking spray.

2. In a small bowl, mix paprika and the remaining salt, rosemary and pepper. Sprinkle chicken with the paprika mixture; arrange over vegetables. Roast until a thermometer inserted in chicken reads 170°-175° and the vegetables are just tender, 35-40 minutes.

3. Remove the chicken to a serving platter; keep warm. Top vegetables with spinach. Roast until vegetables are tender and spinach is wilted, 8-10 minutes longer. Stir vegetables to combine; serve with chicken.

1 CHICKEN THIGH WITH 1 CUP VEGETABLES: 357 cal., 14g fat (3g sat. fat), 87mg chol., 597mg sod., 28g carb. (3g sugars, 4g fiber), 28g pro. *Diabetic exchanges:* 4 lean meat, 1½ starch, 1 vegetable, 1 fat.

COD & ASPARAGUS BAKE

The bright taste of lemon pulls this flavorful and healthy dish together.
You can also use grated Parmesan cheese instead of Romano.
— *Thomas Faglon, Somerset, NJ*

TAKES: 30 min. • **MAKES:** 4 servings

4 cod fillets (4 oz. each)
1 lb. fresh thin
   asparagus, trimmed
1 pint cherry
   tomatoes, halved
2 Tbsp. lemon juice
1½ tsp. grated lemon zest
¼ cup grated
   Romano cheese

1. Preheat oven to 375°. Place cod and asparagus in a 15x10x1-in. baking pan brushed with oil. Add tomatoes, cut side down. Brush fish with lemon juice; sprinkle with lemon zest. Sprinkle fish and vegetables with Romano cheese. Bake until the fish just begins to flake easily with a fork, about 12 minutes.

2. Remove pan from oven; preheat broiler. Broil the cod mixture 3-4 in. from heat until the vegetables are lightly browned, 2-3 minutes.

1 SERVING: 141 cal., 3g fat (2g sat. fat), 45mg chol., 184mg sod., 6g carb. (3g sugars, 2g fiber), 23g pro.
Diabetic exchanges: 3 lean meat, 1 vegetable.

ORANGE-GLAZED PORK WITH SWEET POTATOES

When it's chilly outside, I like to roast pork tenderloin with sweet potatoes, apples and an orange. The sweetness and spices make any evening cozy.
—Danielle Lee Boyles, Weston, WI

PREP: 20 min. • **BAKE:** 55 min. + standing • **MAKES:** 6 servings

1 lb. sweet potatoes (about 2 medium)
2 medium apples
1 medium orange
1 tsp. salt
½ tsp. pepper
1 cup orange juice
2 Tbsp. brown sugar
2 tsp. cornstarch
1 tsp. ground cinnamon
1 tsp. ground ginger
2 pork tenderloins (about 1 lb. each)

1. Preheat oven to 350°. Peel the sweet potatoes; core apples. Cut potatoes, apples and orange crosswise into ¼-in.-thick slices. Arrange in a foil-lined 15x10x1-in. baking pan coated with cooking spray; sprinkle with salt and pepper. Roast 10 minutes.

2. Meanwhile, in a microwave-safe bowl, mix orange juice, brown sugar, cornstarch, cinnamon and ginger. Microwave, covered, on high, stirring every 30 seconds until thickened, 1-2 minutes. Stir until smooth.

3. Place the pork tenderloins over the sweet potato mixture; drizzle with the orange juice mixture. Roast until a thermometer inserted in pork reads 145° and sweet potatoes and apples are tender, 45-55 minutes longer. Remove from oven; tent with foil. Let stand 10 minutes before slicing.

4 OZ. COOKED PORK WITH ABOUT 1 CUP SWEET POTATO MIXTURE: 325 cal., 5g fat (2g sat. fat), 85mg chol., 467mg sod., 36g carb. (21g sugars, 3g fiber), 32g pro. *Diabetic exchanges:* 4 lean meat, 2 starch.

CHAPTER 2

SKILLET

Work some magic on the stovetop with these tasty skillet suppers that make any weeknight dinner a breeze.

Tasty Turkey Skillet 40

Sausage & Vegetable Skillet Dinner 43

Chicken Burrito Skillet. 44

Shrimp Risotto 47

Chicken & Orzo Skillet. 48

Blackened Tilapia with Zucchini Noodles 51

Mahi Mahi & Veggie Skillet. 52

Mom's Paella. 55

Wasabi Beef Fajitas 56

Tomato-Poached Halibut 59

Chicken Veggie Skillet. 60

Cranberry Sweet & Sour Pork 63

Skillet Zucchini & Sausage 64

Mediterranean Spinach & Beans 67

Skillet BBQ Beef Potpie. 68

Cacciatore Chicken Breasts 71

Black Bean & Corn Quinoa. 72

Pierogi Beef Skillet. 75

Cilantro Shrimp & Rice 76

Chicken Thighs with Shallots & Spinach 79

TASTY TURKEY SKILLET

I like to use boxed rice and pasta mixes to jump-start quick meals. This colorful dish is simple to cook on the stovetop using fried rice mix, tender turkey and convenient frozen vegetables.

—*Betty Kleberger, Florissant, MO*

PREP: 10 min. • **COOK:** 35 min. • **MAKES:** 4 servings

1 lb. turkey breast tenderloins, cut into ¼-in. strips
1 pkg. (6.2 oz.) fried rice mix
1 Tbsp. butter
2 cups water
⅛ tsp. cayenne pepper
1½ cups frozen corn, thawed
1 cup frozen broccoli cuts, thawed
2 Tbsp. chopped sweet red pepper, optional

1. In a skillet coated with cooking spray, cook turkey over medium heat until no longer pink; drain. Remove from pan and keep warm.

2. Set aside seasoning packet from rice. In the same skillet, saute rice in butter until lightly browned. Stir in the water, cayenne and contents of seasoning packet.

3. Bring to a boil. Reduce heat; cover and simmer for 15 minutes. Stir in the corn, broccoli, red pepper if desired, and turkey. Return to a boil. Reduce heat; cover and simmer until the rice and vegetables are tender, 6-8 minutes.

1¼ CUPS: 351 cal., 6g fat (2g sat. fat), 53mg chol., 971mg sod., 43g carb. (4g sugars, 4g fiber), 35g pro.

SAUSAGE & VEGETABLE SKILLET DINNER

I threw this together one night to use up produce before going out of town. Who knew it was going to be such a hit? Now it's a recipe I turn to whenever time is tight.

—*Elizabeth Kelley, Chicago, IL*

TAKES: 30 min. • **MAKES:** 4 servings

1 Tbsp. olive oil
1 pkg. (12 oz.) fully cooked Italian chicken sausage links, cut into 1-in. pieces
1 large onion, chopped
3 garlic cloves, minced
¼ tsp. crushed red pepper flakes
1½ lbs. red potatoes (about 5 medium), thinly sliced
1 pkg. (10 oz.) frozen corn
¼ tsp. pepper
1¼ cups vegetable broth
2 cups fresh baby spinach

1. In a 12-in. skillet, heat oil over medium-high heat; saute sausage and onion until the onion is tender. Add garlic and pepper flakes; cook and stir 1 minute.

2. Add potatoes, corn, pepper and broth; bring to a boil. Reduce heat to medium; cook, covered, until the potatoes are tender, 15-20 minutes. Stir in spinach until wilted.

1½ CUPS: 371 cal., 11g fat (3g sat. fat), 65mg chol., 715mg sod., 48g carb. (6g sugars, 5g fiber), 22g pro. *Diabetic exchanges:* 3 starch, 3 lean meat, 1 fat.

HEALTH TIP: Italian chicken sausage has less than half the fat of regular. It's lean, but it adds a lot of flavor.

CHICKEN BURRITO SKILLET

We love Mexican night at our house, and I love to re-create
dishes from our favorite restaurants. This burrito-inspired dish
is ready for the table in almost no time!

—*Krista Marshall, Fort Wayne, IN*

PREP: 15 min. • **COOK:** 30 min. • **MAKES:** 6 servings

1 lb. boneless skinless chicken breasts, cut into 1½-in. pieces
⅛ tsp. salt
⅛ tsp. pepper
2 Tbsp. olive oil, divided
1 cup uncooked long grain rice
1 can (15 oz.) black beans, rinsed and drained
1 can (14½ oz.) diced tomatoes, drained
1 tsp. ground cumin
½ tsp. onion powder
½ tsp. garlic powder
½ tsp. chili powder
2½ cups reduced-sodium chicken broth
1 cup shredded Mexican cheese blend
1 medium tomato, chopped
3 green onions, chopped

1. Toss chicken with salt and pepper. In a large cast-iron or other heavy skillet, heat 1 Tbsp. oil over medium-high heat; saute chicken until browned, about 2 minutes. Remove from pan.

2. In same pan, heat remaining oil over medium-high heat; saute rice until lightly browned, 1-2 minutes. Stir in beans, canned tomatoes, seasonings and broth; bring to a boil. Place chicken on top (do not stir into rice). Simmer, covered, until rice is tender and chicken is no longer pink, 20-25 minutes.

3. Remove from heat; sprinkle with cheese. Let stand, covered, until cheese is melted. Top with tomato and green onions.

1⅓ CUPS: 403 cal., 13g fat (4g sat. fat), 58mg chol., 690mg sod., 43g carb. (4g sugars, 5g fiber), 27g pro. *Diabetic exchanges:* 3 starch, 3 lean meat, 1½ fat.

✳ TEST KITCHEN TIP

Any can of beans in your pantry will work well in this recipe. We particularly like pintos and kidney beans here. Bump up the health factor by using brown rice instead of white.

SHRIMP RISOTTO

This delightful main dish adds elegance to family meals. Instant rice makes it come together quickly for a special dinner any day of the week.
—Taste of Home *Test Kitchen*

TAKES: 30 min. • **MAKES:** 4 servings

1 small onion, chopped
2 Tbsp. butter
1¾ cups uncooked
    instant rice
2 garlic cloves, minced
½ tsp. dried basil
¼ tsp. pepper
2 cans (14½ oz. each)
    chicken broth
1 lb. peeled and deveined
    cooked medium shrimp
2 cups fresh baby spinach,
    coarsely chopped
1 cup frozen corn, thawed
1 plum tomato, chopped
¼ cup grated
    Parmesan cheese
2 Tbsp. 2% milk

1. In a large skillet, saute onion in butter until tender. Add the rice, garlic, basil and pepper; cook 2 minutes longer. Stir in 1 can of broth. Cook and stir until most of the liquid is absorbed.

2. Add remaining broth, ½ cup at a time, stirring constantly. Allow the liquid to absorb between additions. Cook until the risotto is creamy and the rice is tender.

3. Add the remaining ingredients; cook and stir until the spinach is wilted and shrimp are heated through.

1⅓ CUPS: 420 cal., 10g fat (5g sat. fat), 197mg chol., 1196mg sod., 49g carb. (3g sugars, 3g fiber), 32g pro.

CHICKEN & ORZO SKILLET

Here's a perfect one-skillet supper that's colorful, healthy, filling and definitely special! Everyone always seems to love the blend of spices, the touch of heat and the sophisticated flavor.

—Kellie Mulleavy, Lambertville, MI

....

PREP: 15 min. • **COOK:** 20 min. • **MAKES:** 4 servings

1 lb. boneless skinless chicken breasts, cut into ½-in. strips
2 tsp. salt-free garlic seasoning blend
1 small onion, chopped
1 Tbsp. olive oil
1 garlic clove, minced
1 can (14½ oz.) diced tomatoes, undrained
1 pkg. (10 oz.) frozen chopped spinach, thawed and squeezed dry
1 cup reduced-sodium chicken broth
¾ cup uncooked orzo pasta
1 tsp. Italian seasoning
⅛ tsp. crushed red pepper flakes, optional
¼ cup grated Parmesan cheese, optional

1. Sprinkle chicken with garlic seasoning blend. In a large cast-iron or other heavy skillet, saute the chicken and onion in oil until the chicken is no longer pink, 5-6 minutes. Add garlic; cook 1 minute longer.

2. Stir in the tomatoes, spinach, broth, orzo, Italian seasoning and, if desired, pepper flakes. Bring to a boil; reduce heat. Cover and simmer until the orzo is tender and the liquid is absorbed, 15-20 minutes. If desired, sprinkle with cheese.

1¼ CUPS: 339 cal., 7g fat (1g sat. fat), 63mg chol., 384mg sod., 38g carb. (6g sugars, 5g fiber), 32g pro. *Diabetic exchanges:* 3 lean meat, 2 starch, 2 vegetable, ½ fat.

BLACKENED TILAPIA WITH ZUCCHINI NOODLES

I love quick and bright meals like this one-skillet wonder. Complement it with zippy pico de gallo, either your own (easy to make it the night before) or premade from the grocery store.
— *Tammy Brownlow, Dallas, TX*

TAKES: 30 min. • **MAKES:** 4 servings

2   large zucchini
    (about 1½ lbs.)
1½ tsp. ground cumin
¾   tsp. salt, divided
½   tsp. smoked paprika
½   tsp. pepper
¼   tsp garlic powder
4   tilapia fillets (6 oz. each)
2   tsp. olive oil
2   garlic cloves, minced
1   cup pico de gallo

1. Trim ends of zucchini. Using a spiralizer, cut zucchini into thin strands.

2. Mix cumin, ½ tsp. salt, smoked paprika, pepper and garlic powder; sprinkle generously onto both sides of the tilapia. In a large nonstick skillet, heat oil over medium-high heat. In batches, cook tilapia until fish just begins to flake easily with a fork, 2-3 minutes per side. Remove from pan; keep warm.

3. In same pan, cook zucchini strands with garlic powder over medium-high heat until zucchini is slightly softened, 1-2 minutes, tossing constantly with tongs (do not overcook). Sprinkle with the remaining salt. Serve with tilapia and pico de gallo.

1 SERVING: 203 cal., 4g fat (1g sat. fat), 83mg chol., 522mg sod., 8g carb. (5g sugars, 2g fiber), 34g pro. *Diabetic exchanges:* 5 lean meat, 1 vegetable, ½ fat.

✽ TEST KITCHEN TIP

If you don't have a spiralizer, cut the zucchini into ribbons using a vegetable peeler. Saute as directed, increasing time as necessary.

MAHI MAHI & VEGGIE SKILLET

Cooking mahi mahi with a mix of vegetables may seem complex,
but I developed this skillet recipe to bring out the wow factor
without the hassle and fuss.
—*Solomon Wang, Arlington, TX*

TAKES: 30 min. • **MAKES:** 4 servings

3 Tbsp. olive oil, divided
4 mahi mahi or salmon
  fillets (6 oz. each)
3 medium sweet
  red peppers, cut
  into thick strips
½ lb. sliced baby
  portobello mushrooms
1 large sweet onion,
  cut into thick rings
  and separated
⅓ cup lemon juice
¾ tsp. salt, divided
½ tsp. pepper
¼ cup minced fresh chives
⅓ cup pine nuts, optional

1. In a large skillet, heat 2 Tbsp. oil over medium-high heat. Add fillets; cook 4-5 minutes on each side or until the fish just begins to flake easily with a fork. Remove from the pan.

2. Add remaining oil, peppers, mushrooms, onion, lemon juice and ¼ tsp. salt. Cook, covered, over medium heat until vegetables are tender, stirring occasionally, 6-8 minutes.

3. Place the fish over the vegetables; sprinkle with pepper and the remaining salt. Cook, covered, 2 minutes longer or until heated through. Sprinkle with chives and, if desired, pine nuts before serving.

1 SERVING: 307 cal., 12g fat (2g sat. fat), 124mg chol., 606mg sod., 15g carb. (9g sugars, 3g fiber), 35g pro. *Diabetic exchanges:* 4 lean meat, 3 vegetable, 2 fat.

MOM'S PAELLA

*I enjoy cooking ethnic foods, especially those that call for lots of rice.
Like my mom, I often prepare this dish for special Sunday get-togethers.
Traditional paella uses saffron, but turmeric is a budget-friendly alternative.*
—*Ena Quiggle, Goodhue, MN*

PREP: 10 min. • **COOK:** 40 min. • **MAKES:** 6-8 servings

1½ cups cubed
cooked chicken
1 cup cubed fully
cooked ham
½ cup sliced fully cooked
smoked sausage
(¼-in. slices)
1 medium onion,
chopped
1 small green pepper,
chopped
4 Tbsp. olive oil, divided
¼ cup pimiento-stuffed
olives, halved
½ cup raisins, optional
1 cup uncooked
converted rice
2 garlic cloves, minced
3 tsp. ground turmeric
1½ tsp. curry powder
2¼ cups chicken broth
1½ cups frozen
mixed vegetables

1. In a large skillet, saute the chicken, ham, sausage, onion and green pepper in 2 Tbsp. oil for 3-5 minutes or until the onion is tender. Add olives and raisins if desired. Cook 2-3 minutes longer or until heated through, stirring occasionally; remove the meat and vegetable mixture from pan and keep warm.

2. In the same skillet, saute rice in remaining oil for 2-3 minutes or until lightly browned. Stir in the garlic, turmeric and curry. Return the meat and vegetable mixture to the pan; toss lightly. Add broth and the mixed vegetables; bring to a boil. Reduce heat; cover and simmer for 25-30 minutes or until rice is tender.

1 CUP: 258 cal., 14g fat (3g sat. fat), 39mg chol., 711mg sod., 19g carb. (3g sugars, 3g fiber), 15g pro.

WASABI BEEF FAJITAS

Beef fajitas get an Eastern spin with gingerroot, sesame oil and wasabi, a type of Japanese horseradish. You can find it in the Asian section at your supermarket.
—Taste of Home *Test Kitchen*

TAKES: 20 min. • **MAKES:** 8 servings

2 tsp. cornstarch
3 Tbsp. reduced-sodium soy sauce
2 tsp. prepared wasabi
2 tsp. minced fresh gingerroot
1 garlic clove, minced
2 Tbsp. sesame oil, divided
1 lb. uncooked beef stir-fry strips
12 green onions with tops, cut in half lengthwise
1 large sweet red pepper, julienned
8 flour tortillas (8 in.), warmed
1 cup coleslaw mix

1. In a small bowl, mix cornstarch, soy sauce, wasabi, ginger and garlic until blended. In a large skillet, heat 1 Tbsp. oil over medium-high heat. Add beef; stir-fry 4-6 minutes or until no longer pink. Remove from pan.

2. Stir-fry green onions and red pepper in remaining oil 2-3 minutes or until vegetables are crisp-tender.

3. Stir cornstarch mixture and add to pan. Bring to a boil; cook and stir 1-2 minutes or until sauce is thickened. Return beef to pan; heat through. Serve with tortillas and coleslaw mix.

1 FAJITA: 287 cal., 9g fat (2g sat. fat), 23mg chol., 507mg sod., 32g carb. (2g sugars, 3g fiber), 17g pro. *Diabetic exchanges:* 2 starch, 2 lean meat, ½ fat.

TOMATO-POACHED HALIBUT

My simple halibut with its tangy tomato sauce and bright burst of lemon comes together in one pan. Try it with polenta, angel hair pasta or crusty bread.
—*Danna Rogers, Westport, CT*

TAKES: 30 min. • **MAKES:** 4 servings

1 Tbsp. olive oil
2 poblano peppers, finely chopped
1 small onion, finely chopped
1 can (14½ oz.) fire-roasted diced tomatoes, undrained
1 can (14½ oz.) no-salt-added diced tomatoes, undrained
¼ cup chopped pitted green olives
3 garlic cloves, minced
¼ tsp. pepper
⅛ tsp. salt
4 halibut fillets (4 oz. each)
⅓ cup chopped fresh cilantro
4 lemon wedges
Crusty whole grain bread, optional

1. In a large nonstick skillet, heat oil over medium-high heat. Add poblano peppers and onion; cook and stir for 4-6 minutes or until tender.

2. Stir in tomatoes, olives, garlic, pepper and salt. Bring to a boil. Adjust heat to maintain a gentle simmer. Add fillets. Cook, covered, 8-10 minutes or until the fish just begins to flake easily with a fork. Sprinkle with cilantro. Serve with lemon wedges and, if desired, bread.

1 FILLET WITH 1 CUP SAUCE: 224 cal., 7g fat (1g sat. fat), 56mg chol., 651mg sod., 17g carb. (8g sugars, 4g fiber), 24g pro. *Diabetic exchanges:* 3 lean meat, 1 starch, ½ fat.

CHICKEN VEGGIE SKILLET

I concocted this chicken and veggie dish one night as a way
to use up extra mushrooms and asparagus. My husband suggested
I write it down because it's a keeper.
—*Rebekah Beyer, Sabetha, KS*

TAKES: 30 min. • **MAKES:** 6 servings

1½ lbs. boneless skinless
   chicken breasts,
   cut into ½-in. strips
½ tsp. salt
¼ tsp. pepper
6 tsp. olive oil, divided
½ lb. sliced fresh
   mushrooms
1 small onion, halved
   and sliced
2 garlic cloves, minced
1 lb. fresh asparagus,
   trimmed and cut
   into 1-in. pieces
½ cup sherry or
   chicken stock
2 Tbsp. cold butter, cubed

1. Sprinkle chicken with salt and pepper. In a large skillet, heat 1 tsp. oil over medium-high heat. Add half of the chicken; cook and stir for 3-4 minutes or until chicken is no longer pink. Remove from pan. Repeat with 1 tsp. oil and the remaining chicken.

2. In same pan, heat 2 tsp. oil. Add mushrooms and onion; cook and stir 2-3 minutes or until tender. Add garlic; cook 1 minute longer. Add to the chicken.

3. Heat the remaining oil in pan. Add asparagus; cook 2-3 minutes or until crisp-tender. Add to the chicken and mushrooms.

4. Add sherry to skillet, stirring to loosen any browned bits from the pan. Bring to a boil; cook 1-2 minutes or until liquid is reduced to 2 Tbsp.. Return the chicken and vegetables to pan; heat through. Remove from heat; stir in butter, 1 Tbsp. at a time.

1 CUP: 228 cal., 11g fat (4g sat. fat), 73mg chol., 384mg sod., 6g carb. (2g sugars, 1g fiber), 25g pro. *Diabetic exchanges:* 3 lean meat, 2 fat, 1 vegetable.

CRANBERRY SWEET & SOUR PORK

This fresh take on the beloved classic is sure to cause a stir at the dinner table as Asian-style cuisine meets North American sweet-tangy cranberries.
—*Gert Snyder, West Montrose, ON*

TAKES: 20 min. • **MAKES:** 6 servings

1 Tbsp. cornstarch
½ cup unsweetened pineapple juice
1 cup whole-berry cranberry sauce
½ cup barbecue sauce
1½ lbs. pork tenderloin, cut into ½-in. cubes
1 Tbsp. canola oil
½ tsp. salt
¼ tsp. pepper
1 medium green pepper, cut into strips
¾ cup pineapple tidbits
Hot cooked rice, chow mein noodles or crispy wonton strips, optional

1. In a small bowl, combine cornstarch and pineapple juice until smooth. Stir in the cranberry and barbecue sauces; set aside.

2. In a large skillet, stir-fry pork in oil for 3 minutes or until the meat is no longer pink. Sprinkle with salt and pepper. Remove from the pan and keep warm.

3. Add green pepper and pineapple to the pan; stir-fry for 2 minutes. Stir the cornstarch mixture and add to the skillet. Bring to a boil. Cook and stir for 2 minutes or until thickened. Add pork; heat through. Serve with rice, noodles or wonton strips if desired.

FREEZE OPTION: Place the cooled meat mixture in freezer containers. To use, partially thaw in refrigerator overnight. Heat through slowly in a covered skillet, stirring occasionally, adding a little water if necessary.

1¼ CUPS: 268 cal., 7g fat (2g sat. fat), 63mg chol., 444mg sod., 28g carb. (19g sugars, 1g fiber), 23g pro.

SKILLET ZUCCHINI & SAUSAGE

I often turn to this dish when folks drop by. It is easy to make and takes little time to prepare. Judging by the requests I receive for the recipe, everyone loves it! This dish goes well with cornbread or garlic bread.

—LaBelle Doster, Vancouver, WA

TAKES: 30 min. • **MAKES:** 10 servings

2 Tbsp. vegetable oil
½ lb. fully cooked smoked Polish sausage, cut into ½-in. diagonal slices
1 cup chopped onion
1 cup sliced celery
½ cup chopped green pepper
1 garlic clove, minced
½ tsp. dried oregano
½ tsp. pepper
4 to 5 medium zucchini, sliced
4 to 5 medium tomatoes, coarsely chopped
Herb seasoning blend to taste

Heat oil in a large skillet over medium-high heat. Lightly brown the sausage. Add onion, celery, green pepper, garlic, oregano and pepper. Cook and stir until the vegetables are almost tender. Add zucchini and tomatoes; cook and stir until zucchini is just tender. Sprinkle with seasoning blend.

1 CUP: 130 cal., 9g fat (3g sat. fat), 16mg chol., 211mg sod., 8g carb. (4g sugars, 2g fiber), 5g pro.

MEDITERRANEAN SPINACH & BEANS

This dish is delicious served either hot or cold. To make it vegetarian, just use soy sauce instead of Worcestershire.
—*Becky Cuba, Spotsylvania, VA*

TAKES: 30 min. • **MAKES:** 4 servings

1 Tbsp. olive oil
1 small onion, chopped
2 garlic cloves, minced
1 can (14½ oz.) no-salt-added diced tomatoes, undrained
2 Tbsp. Worcestershire sauce
¼ tsp. salt
¼ tsp. pepper
⅛ tsp. crushed red pepper flakes
1 can (15 oz.) cannellini beans, rinsed and drained
1 can (14 oz.) water-packed artichoke hearts, rinsed, drained and quartered
6 oz. fresh baby spinach (about 8 cups)
  Additional olive oil, optional

1. In a 12-in. skillet, heat oil over medium-high heat; saute onion until tender, 3-5 minutes. Add garlic; cook and stir 1 minute. Stir in tomatoes, Worcestershire sauce and seasonings; bring to a boil. Reduce heat; simmer, uncovered, until liquid is almost evaporated, 6-8 minutes.

2. Add beans, artichoke hearts and spinach; cook and stir until the spinach is wilted, 3-5 minutes. If desired, drizzle with additional oil.

1½ CUPS: 187 cal., 4g fat (1g sat. fat), 0 chol., 650mg sod., 30g carb. (4g sugars, 6g fiber), 8g pro. *Diabetic exchanges:* 1 starch, 1 lean meat, 2 vegetable, 1 fat.

SKILLET BBQ BEEF POTPIE

Beef potpie is a classic comfort food, but who's got time to see it through? My crowd-pleasing stovetop version is speedy and convenient; it's also an excellent way to use up leftover stuffing.
—*Priscilla Yee, Concord, CA*

TAKES: 25 min. • **MAKES:** 4 servings

1 lb. lean ground beef (90% lean)
⅓ cup thinly sliced green onions, divided
2 cups frozen mixed vegetables, thawed
½ cup salsa
½ cup barbecue sauce
3 cups cooked cornbread stuffing
½ cup shredded cheddar cheese
¼ cup chopped sweet red pepper

1. In a large skillet, cook beef and ¼ cup of the green onions over medium heat for 6-8 minutes or until the beef is no longer pink, breaking into crumbles; drain. Stir in mixed vegetables, salsa and barbecue sauce; cook, covered, over medium-low heat for 4-5 minutes or until heated through.

2. Layer stuffing over the beef; sprinkle with cheese, red pepper and the remaining green onion. Cook, covered, 3-5 minutes longer or until heated through and cheese is melted.

1½ CUPS: 634 cal., 27g fat (9g sat. fat), 85mg chol., 1372mg sod., 62g carb. (19g sugars, 9g fiber), 33g pro.

CACCIATORE CHICKEN BREASTS

This easy recipe is my version of traditional chicken cacciatore.
The tasty sauce and chicken can be served over rice or noodles. If you want
to lower the sodium content, use garlic powder instead of garlic salt.
—*JoAnn McCauley, Dubuque, IA*

TAKES: 30 min. • **MAKES:** 2 servings

½ medium onion, sliced
  and separated into rings
½ medium green
  pepper, sliced
1 Tbsp. olive oil
2 boneless skinless
  chicken breast halves
  (5 oz. each)
¾ cup canned
  stewed tomatoes
2 Tbsp. white wine
  or chicken broth
¼ tsp. garlic salt
¼ tsp. dried
  rosemary, crushed
⅛ tsp. pepper

1. In a large skillet, saute onion and green pepper in oil until crisp-tender. Remove and keep warm. Cook the chicken over medium-high heat until juices run clear, 4-5 minutes on each side. Remove and set aside.

2. Add tomatoes, wine, garlic salt, rosemary and pepper to the skillet. Stir in the onion mixture and heat through. Serve with chicken.

1 CHICKEN BREAST HALF WITH ¾ CUP SAUCE:
272 cal., 10g fat (2g sat. fat), 78mg chol., 462mg sod., 12g carb. (7g sugars, 2g fiber), 30g pro. *Diabetic exchanges:* 4 lean meat, 2 vegetable, 1½ fat.

BLACK BEAN & CORN QUINOA

My daughter's college asked parents to send in suggestions for a favorite healthy recipe to use in the dining halls. This quinoa fits the bill, and gives my daughter a taste of home!
—*Lindsay McSweeney, Winchester, MA*

TAKES: 30 min. • **MAKES:** 4 servings

2 Tbsp. canola oil
1 medium onion, finely chopped
1 medium sweet red pepper, finely chopped
1 celery rib, finely chopped
2 tsp. chili powder
¼ tsp. salt
¼ tsp. pepper
2 cups vegetable stock
1 cup frozen corn
1 cup quinoa, rinsed
1 can (15 oz.) black beans, rinsed and drained
⅓ cup plus 2 Tbsp. minced fresh cilantro, divided

1. In a large skillet, heat oil over medium-high heat. Add onion, red pepper, celery and seasonings; cook and stir 5-7 minutes or until the vegetables are tender.

2. Stir in stock and corn; bring to a boil. Stir in quinoa. Reduce heat; simmer, covered, for 12-15 minutes or until the liquid is absorbed.

3. Add beans and ⅓ cup cilantro; heat through, stirring occasionally. Sprinkle with the remaining cilantro.

NOTE: Look for quinoa in the cereal, rice or organic food aisle.

1¼ CUPS: 375 cal., 10g fat (1g sat. fat), 0 chol., 668mg sod., 60g carb. (5g sugars, 10g fiber), 13g pro.

PIEROGI BEEF SKILLET

Hearty and thick with beef, veggies and potatoes, this is a complete meal in one—delicious, easy to make and utterly satisfying.
—Taste of Home *Test Kitchen*

TAKES: 25 min. • **MAKES:** 4 servings

1 lb. ground beef
½ cup chopped onion
¼ cup all-purpose flour
½ tsp. Italian seasoning
½ tsp. pepper
⅛ tsp. salt
1 can (14½ oz.) beef broth
1 pkg. (16 oz.) frozen cheese and potato pierogi, thawed
2 cups frozen mixed vegetables (about 10 oz.), thawed and drained
½ cup shredded cheddar cheese

1. In a large cast-iron or other heavy skillet, cook and crumble beef with onion over medium heat until the meat is no longer pink, 5-7 minutes; drain, reserving 3 Tbsp. drippings. Stir in flour and seasonings until blended. Gradually stir in broth; bring to a boil. Cook and stir until thickened, 1-2 minutes.

2. Stir in pierogi and vegetables. Cook, uncovered, until heated through, about 5 minutes, stirring occasionally. Sprinkle with cheese.

1¾ CUPS: 654 cal., 31g fat (12g sat. fat), 102mg chol., 1157mg sod., 57g carb. (12g sugars, 7g fiber), 34g pro.

CILANTRO SHRIMP & RICE

I created this dish especially for my son, who has the pickiest palate. The aroma of fresh herbs is so appetizing—even he can't resist!
—Nibedita Das, Fort Worth, TX

TAKES: 30 min. • **MAKES:** 8 servings

2 pkg. (8½ oz. each) ready-to-serve basmati rice
2 Tbsp. olive oil
2 cups frozen corn, thawed
2 medium zucchini, quartered and sliced
1 large sweet red pepper, chopped
½ tsp. crushed red pepper flakes
3 garlic cloves, minced
1 lb. peeled and deveined cooked large shrimp, tails removed
½ cup chopped fresh cilantro
1 Tbsp. grated lime zest
2 Tbsp. lime juice
¾ tsp. salt
Lime wedges, optional

1. Prepare rice according to the package directions.

2. Meanwhile, in a large skillet, heat olive oil over medium-high heat. Add corn, zucchini, red pepper and pepper flakes; cook and stir 3-5 minutes or until the zucchini is crisp-tender. Add garlic; cook 1 minute longer. Add shrimp; cook and stir 3-5 minutes or until heated through.

3. Stir in the rice, cilantro, lime zest, lime juice and salt. If desired, serve with lime wedges.

1½ CUPS: 243 cal., 6g fat (1g sat. fat), 86mg chol., 324mg sod., 28g carb. (3g sugars, 3g fiber), 16g pro. *Diabetic exchanges:* 2 lean meat, 1½ starch, ½ fat.

CHICKEN THIGHS WITH SHALLOTS & SPINACH

What could be better than an entree that comes with its own creamy vegetable side? It makes an appealing presentation and goes together in no time flat for a healthy supper.
—*Genna Johannes, Wrightstown, WI*

TAKES: 30 min. • **MAKES:** 6 servings

6 boneless skinless chicken thighs (about 1½ lbs.)
½ tsp. seasoned salt
½ tsp. pepper
1½ tsp. olive oil
4 shallots, thinly sliced
⅓ cup white wine or reduced-sodium chicken broth
1 pkg. (10 oz.) fresh spinach, trimmed
¼ tsp. salt
¼ cup reduced-fat sour cream

1. Sprinkle chicken with seasoned salt and pepper. In a large skillet coated with cooking spray, heat oil over medium heat. Add the chicken; cook until a thermometer reads 170°, about 6 minutes on each side. Remove from pan; keep warm.

2. In the same pan, cook and stir sliced shallots until tender. Add wine; bring to a boil. Cook until the wine is reduced by half. Add the spinach and salt; cook and stir just until spinach is wilted. Stir in sour cream; serve with the chicken.

FREEZE OPTION: Before adding sour cream, cool chicken and spinach mixture. Freeze in freezer containers. To use, partially thaw in refrigerator overnight. Heat through slowly in a covered skillet until a thermometer inserted in chicken reads 165°, stirring occasionally. Stir in sour cream.

1 CHICKEN THIGH WITH ¼ CUP SPINACH MIXTURE: 223 cal., 10g fat (3g sat. fat), 77mg chol., 360mg sod., 7g carb. (2g sugars, 1g fiber), 23g pro. *Diabetic exchanges:* 3 lean meat, 1½ fat, 1 vegetable.

LAMB STEW, 101

CHAPTER 3

DUTCH OVEN

A Dutch oven goes smoothly from stovetop to oven, making some of the most classic and hearty meals possible.

Cazuela 82

Fire-Roasted Ziti with Sausage 85

Spanish Rice with Chicken & Peas 86

Pasta & Broccoli Sausage Simmer 89

Seafood Gumbo 90

Stout & Shiitake Pot Roast 93

Hearty Brunswick Stew 94

One-Pot Spaghetti Dinner 97

Easy Chicken & Dumplings 98

Lamb Stew 101

Inside-Out Stuffed Cabbage 102

Favorite Hamburger Stew 105

Savory Braised Chicken with Vegetables 106

Turkey Dumpling Stew 109

Slow-Simmered Burgundy Beef Stew 110

Veg Jambalaya 113

Sunday Cassoulet 114

Chicken Chili with Black Beans 117

Creole Jambalaya 118

Sausage & Kale Lentil Stew 121

Stovetop Tarragon Chicken 122

CAZUELA

I learned to make this dish while we were living in Chile for a few months. Now, back in the States, we grow extra butternut squash in our garden just for this recipe.
—*Louise Schmid, Marshall, MN*

PREP: 20 min. • **COOK:** 30 min. • **MAKES:** 6 servings

6   chicken drumsticks
    or thighs
3   cups cubed peeled
    butternut squash
    (1-in. cubes)
6   small potatoes, peeled
6   pieces of fresh or
    frozen corn on the cob
    (2 in. each)
3   carrots, cut into
    1-in. chunks
3   cans (14½ oz. each)
    chicken broth
    Hot cooked rice
    Hot pepper sauce
    to taste
    Salt and pepper to taste
    Minced fresh cilantro
    or parsley

1. Place the chicken, squash, potatoes, corn, carrots and broth in a large soup kettle or Dutch oven; bring to a boil. Reduce heat; cover and simmer 25 minutes or until the chicken is done and vegetables are tender.

2. Serve over rice in a shallow soup bowl. Serve with hot pepper sauce, salt, pepper and cilantro or parsley.

1 SERVING: 416 cal., 8g fat (2g sat. fat), 52mg chol., 968mg sod., 67g carb. (12g sugars, 8g fiber), 23g pro.

FIRE-ROASTED ZITI WITH SAUSAGE

We punch up our pasta with smoked sausage and fire-roasted tomato sauce. It's an easy recipe to switch up—use whatever noodles or spaghetti sauce is in your pantry.

—*Jean Komlos, Plymouth, MI*

TAKES: 30 min. • **MAKES:** 8 servings

8 oz. uncooked ziti or rigatoni (about 3 cups)
1 can (28 oz.) Italian diced tomatoes, drained
1 jar (24 oz.) fire-roasted tomato and garlic pasta sauce
1 pkg. (16 oz.) smoked sausage, sliced
2 cups shredded part-skim mozzarella cheese, divided
1 cup 4% cottage cheese

1. In a Dutch oven, cook ziti according to the package directions for al dente. Drain; return to pot.

2. Add tomatoes, pasta sauce and sausage to the ziti; heat through over medium heat, stirring occasionally. Stir in 1 cup mozzarella cheese and cottage cheese. Sprinkle with the remaining mozzarella cheese. Cook, covered, 2-5 minutes or until cheese is melted.

1¼ CUPS: 463 cal., 23g fat (11g sat. fat), 66mg chol., 1634mg sod., 41g carb. (15g sugars, 3g fiber), 23g pro.

SPANISH RICE WITH CHICKEN & PEAS

This dish reminds me of my wonderful family dinners growing up. My mom made this juicy chicken and rice for us every Wednesday, and now I make it for my family.
—*Josee Lanzi, New Port Richey, FL*

PREP: 15 min. • **COOK:** 30 min. • **MAKES:** 6 servings

1 lb. boneless skinless chicken breasts, cut into 1½-in. pieces
1 Tbsp. all-purpose flour
½ tsp. pepper
½ tsp. salt, divided
4 tsp. plus 1 Tbsp. olive oil, divided
1 small sweet red pepper, chopped
1 small onion, chopped
1 celery rib, chopped
1½ cups uncooked long grain rice
1 tsp. ground cumin
1 tsp. chili powder
2¼ cups chicken broth
1 can (14½ oz.) diced tomatoes, undrained
1 cup frozen peas, thawed

1. In a small bowl, toss chicken with flour, pepper and ¼ tsp. salt. In a Dutch oven, heat 4 tsp. oil over medium-high heat. Brown chicken pieces, stirring occasionally; remove from pot.

2. In same pot, heat the remaining oil over medium heat. Add pepper, onion and celery; cook and stir until onion is tender, 2-4 minutes. Add the rice, cumin, chili powder and remaining salt; stir to coat rice. Stir in the remaining ingredients; bring to a boil. Reduce heat; simmer, covered, 10 minutes.

3. Place browned chicken over rice (do not stir in). Cook, covered, until rice is tender and chicken is cooked through, about 5 minutes longer.

1½ CUPS: 367 cal., 8g fat (1g sat. fat), 44mg chol., 755mg sod., 50g carb. (5g sugars, 4g fiber), 22g pro. *Diabetic exchanges:* 3 starch, 2 lean meat, 1 vegetable, 1 fat.

PASTA & BROCCOLI SAUSAGE SIMMER

I created this meal when trying to use up a large head of broccoli.
My family requests it at least once a week, which is handy
because we always have the ingredients!
—*Lisa Montgomery, Elmira, ON*

TAKES: 30 min. • **MAKES:** 8 servings

3 cups uncooked
    spiral pasta
2 lbs. smoked kielbasa
    or Polish sausage,
    cut into ¼-in. slices
2 medium bunches
    broccoli, cut into florets
1 cup sliced red onion
2 cans (14½ oz. each) diced
    tomatoes, undrained
2 Tbsp. minced fresh basil
    or 2 tsp. dried basil
2 Tbsp. minced fresh
    parsley or 2 tsp. dried
    parsley flakes
2 tsp. sugar

1. Cook pasta according to package directions.

2. Meanwhile, in a Dutch oven, saute the sausage, broccoli and onion until the broccoli is crisp-tender, 5-6 minutes.

3. Add the tomatoes, basil, parsley and sugar. Cover and simmer for 10 minutes. Drain pasta; stir into the sausage mixture.

1 SERVING: 544 cal., 32g fat (11g sat. fat), 76mg chol., 1395mg sod., 42g carb. (9g sugars, 8g fiber), 25g pro.

SEAFOOD GUMBO

Gumbo helped make Louisiana cuisine famous. We live across the state line in Texas and can't get enough of this traditional Cajun dish. This recipe calls for seafood, but you could also use chicken, duck or sausage.

—*Ruth Aubey, San Antonio, TX*

PREP: 20 min. • **COOK:** 30 min. • **MAKES:** about 6 qt.

1 cup all-purpose flour
1 cup canola oil
4 cups chopped onion
2 cups chopped celery
2 cups chopped green pepper
1 cup sliced green onion and tops
4 cups chicken broth
8 cups water
4 cups sliced okra
2 Tbsp. paprika
2 Tbsp. salt
2 tsp. oregano
1 tsp. ground black pepper
6 cups small shrimp, rinsed and drained, or seafood of your choice
1 cup minced fresh parsley
2 Tbsp. Cajun seasoning

1. In a heavy Dutch oven, combine flour and oil until smooth. Cook over medium-high heat for 5 minutes, stirring constantly. Reduce heat to medium. Cook and stir about 10 minutes more, or until mixture is reddish brown.

2. Add the onion, celery, green pepper and green onions; cook and stir for 5 minutes. Add the chicken broth, water, okra, paprika, salt, oregano and pepper. Bring to boil; reduce heat and simmer, covered, for 10 minutes.

3. Add shrimp and parsley. Simmer, uncovered, about 5 minutes more or until the seafood is done. Remove from heat; stir in Cajun seasoning.

1 CUP: 175 cal., 9g fat (1g sat. fat), 115mg chol., 1574mg sod., 10g carb. (3g sugars, 2g fiber), 12g pro.

STOUT & SHIITAKE POT ROAST

Mushrooms, onions and a bottle of Guinness add excellent flavor to my pot roast. This one-dish wonder tastes even better the next day.
—*Madeleine Bessette, Coeur d'Alene, ID*

PREP: 30 min. • **COOK:** 1¾ hours • **MAKES:** 6 servings

3 Tbsp. olive oil, divided
1 boneless beef chuck roast (2 to 3 lbs.)
2 medium onions, sliced
1 garlic clove, minced
1 bottle (12 oz.) stout or nonalcoholic beer
½ oz. dried shiitake mushrooms (about ½ cup)
1 Tbsp. brown sugar
1 tsp. Worcestershire sauce
½ tsp. dried savory
1 lb. red potatoes (about 8 small), cut into 1-in. pieces
2 medium carrots, sliced
½ cup water
½ tsp. salt
¼ tsp. pepper

1. In a Dutch oven, heat 1 Tbsp. oil over medium heat. Brown roast on all sides; remove from pan.

2. In same pot, heat the remaining oil. Add onions and garlic; cook and stir until tender. Add beer, stirring to loosen browned bits from pot. Stir in mushrooms, brown sugar, Worcestershire sauce and savory. Return roast to the pot. Bring to a boil. Reduce heat; simmer, covered, for 1½ hours.

3. Stir in the remaining ingredients. Return to a boil. Reduce heat; simmer, covered, 15-25 minutes longer or until the meat and vegetables are tender. If desired, skim fat and thicken cooking juices for gravy.

4 OZ. COOKED BEEF WITH 1 CUP VEGETABLES: 441 cal., 21g fat (7g sat. fat), 98mg chol., 293mg sod., 24g carb. (9g sugars, 3g fiber), 33g pro.

HEARTY BRUNSWICK STEW

This thick stew is filled to the brim with a bounty of potatoes, lima beans, corn and tomatoes. Authentic versions call for rabbit or squirrel, but I think you'll love the tender chunks of chicken.

—Mildred Sherrer, Fort Worth, TX

PREP: 1 hour + cooling • **COOK:** 45 min. • **MAKES:** 6 servings

1 broiler/fryer chicken (3½ to 4 lbs.), cut up
2 cups water
4 medium potatoes, peeled and cubed
2 medium onions, sliced
1 can (15¼ oz.) lima beans, rinsed and drained
1 tsp. salt
½ tsp. pepper
Dash cayenne pepper
1 can (15¼ oz.) corn, drained
1 can (14½ oz.) diced tomatoes, undrained
¼ cup butter
½ cup dry bread crumbs

1. In a Dutch oven, slowly bring the chicken and water to a boil. Cover and simmer for 45-60 minutes or until chicken is tender, skimming the surface as foam rises.

2. Remove chicken and set aside until cool enough to handle. Remove and discard skin and bones. Cube chicken and return to the pot.

3. Add the potatoes, onions, beans and seasonings. Bring to a boil. Reduce heat; simmer, uncovered, for 30 minutes or until the potatoes are tender. Stir in the remaining ingredients. Simmer, uncovered, for 10 minutes or until slightly thickened. Serve from Dutch oven or transfer to a serving dish.

1 SERVING: 589 cal., 25g fat (9g sat. fat), 123mg chol., 1147mg sod., 47g carb. (9g sugars, 7g fiber), 40g pro.

ONE-POT SPAGHETTI DINNER

All you need is one pot to make this meal that features a simple and savory homemade sauce. Allspice adds a distinctive flavor, but you can substitute Italian seasoning if you prefer.
—*Carol Benzel-Schmidt, Stanwood, WA*

PREP: 10 min. • **COOK:** 25 min. • **MAKES:** 4 servings

1   lb. lean ground beef (90% lean)
1¾ cups sliced fresh mushrooms
3   cups tomato juice
1   can (14½ oz.) no-salt-added diced tomatoes, drained
1   can (8 oz.) no-salt-added tomato sauce
1   Tbsp. dried minced onion
½   tsp. salt
½   tsp. garlic powder
½   tsp. ground mustard
¼   tsp. pepper
⅛   tsp. ground allspice
⅛   tsp. ground mace, optional
6   oz. uncooked multigrain spaghetti, broken into pieces
    Fresh mozzarella cheese pearls or shaved Parmesan cheese, optional

1. In a Dutch oven, cook beef and mushrooms over medium heat until the meat is no longer pink; drain. Add tomato juice, tomatoes, tomato sauce, onion and seasonings.

2. Bring to a boil. Stir in spaghetti. Simmer, covered, 12-15 minutes or until the spaghetti is tender. If desired, serve with cheese.

1½ CUPS: 414 cal., 10g fat (4g sat. fat), 71mg chol., 925mg sod., 48g carb. (15g sugars, 6g fiber), 33g pro.

EASY CHICKEN & DUMPLINGS

Perfect for fall nights, my simple version of comforting chicken and dumplings is speedy, low in fat and a delicious one-dish meal.
—*Nancy Tuck, Elk Falls, KS*

TAKES: 30 min. • **MAKES:** 6 servings

3 celery ribs, chopped
2 medium carrots, sliced
3 cans (14½ oz. each) reduced-sodium chicken broth
3 cups cubed cooked chicken breast
½ tsp. poultry seasoning
⅛ tsp. pepper
1⅔ cups reduced-fat biscuit/baking mix
⅔ cup fat-free milk

1. In a Dutch oven coated with cooking spray, cook and stir celery and carrots over medium heat until tender, about 5 minutes. Stir in broth, chicken, poultry seasoning and pepper. Bring to a boil; reduce heat to a gentle simmer.

2. For the dumplings, mix biscuit mix and milk until a soft dough forms. Drop by tablespoonfuls on top of the simmering liquid. Reduce heat to low; cover and cook until a toothpick inserted in dumplings comes out clean (do not lift cover during the first 10 minutes), 10-15 minutes.

1 CUP: 260 cal., 4g fat (1g sat. fat), 54mg chol., 964mg sod., 28g carb. (6g sugars, 2g fiber), 27g pro.

LAMB STEW

My grandmother used to make this stew as a special Sunday meal.
It's also a memorable treat from Ireland. If you like your stew
thick and rich, you've got to try this!
—*Vickie Desourdy, WA, NC*

PREP: 40 min. • **BAKE:** 1½ hours • **MAKES:** 8 servings (2½ qt.)

2 lbs. lamb stew meat, cut into 1-in. cubes
1 Tbsp. butter
1 Tbsp. olive oil
1 lb. carrots, sliced
2 medium onions, thinly sliced
2 garlic cloves, minced
1½ cups reduced-sodium chicken broth
1 bottle (12 oz.) Guinness stout or additional reduced-sodium chicken broth
6 medium red potatoes, peeled and cut into 1-in. cubes
4 bay leaves
2 fresh thyme sprigs
2 fresh rosemary sprigs
2 tsp. salt
1½ tsp. pepper
¼ cup heavy whipping cream

1. Preheat oven to 325°. In an ovenproof Dutch oven, brown lamb in butter and oil in batches. Remove and keep warm. In the same pan, saute carrots and onions in the drippings until crisp-tender. Add garlic; cook 1 minute. Gradually add broth and beer. Stir in the lamb, potatoes, bay leaves, thyme, rosemary, salt and pepper.

2. Cover and bake for 1½-2 hours or until the meat and vegetables are tender, stirring every 30 minutes. Discard bay leaves, thyme and rosemary. Stir in cream; heat through.

FREEZE OPTION: Place individual portions of stew in freezer containers and freeze up to 3 months. To use, partially thaw in refrigerator overnight. Heat through in a saucepan, stirring occasionally and adding a little water if necessary.

1¼ CUPS: 311 cal., 12g fat (5g sat. fat), 88mg chol., 829mg sod., 23g carb. (6g sugars, 4g fiber), 26g pro. *Diabetic exchanges:* 3 lean meat, 2 vegetable, 1 starch, 1 fat.

INSIDE-OUT STUFFED CABBAGE

Making stuffed cabbage can be time-consuming, but this version is table-ready in just 30 minutes—and it's got all the classic flavors, plus butternut squash.
—Taste of Home *Test Kitchen*

PREP: 10 min. • **COOK:** 25 min. • **MAKES:** 4 servings

1 lb. ground beef
2 cups cubed peeled butternut squash (about 12 oz.)
1 medium green pepper, chopped
1 envelope Lipton beefy onion soup mix
1 Tbsp. brown sugar
1 can (11½ oz.) Spicy Hot V8 juice
1 cup water
6 cups chopped cabbage (about 1 small head)
½ cup uncooked instant brown rice

1. In a Dutch oven, cook and crumble beef with squash and pepper over medium-high heat until meat is no longer pink; drain. Stir in soup mix, brown sugar, V8 juice, water and cabbage; bring to a boil. Reduce heat; simmer, covered, until cabbage is tender, 8-10 minutes, stirring occasionally.

2. Stir in rice; return to a boil. Simmer, covered, for 5 minutes. Remove from heat; let stand, covered, until rice is tender, about 5 minutes.

1½ CUPS: 382 cal., 15g fat (5g sat. fat), 70mg chol., 841mg sod., 40g carb. (13g sugars, 7g fiber), 25g pro.

✱ TEST KITCHEN TIP

Cut prep time by using frozen already cubed butternut squash. If you like cabbage rolls a little on the sour side, add a tablespoon or two of white or cider vinegar at the end of the cook time.

FAVORITE HAMBURGER STEW

I got this recipe from a woman at our church when I needed a way to use up our bounty of home-canned tomatoes. My husband loves it, and I like that it's easy to warm up for a carefree dinner in the winter months.
—*Marcia Clay, Truman, MN*

PREP: 20 min. • **COOK:** 65 min. • **MAKES:** 4 qt.

- 2 lbs. ground beef
- 2 medium onions, chopped
- 4 cans (14½ oz. each) stewed tomatoes, undrained
- 8 medium carrots, thinly sliced
- 4 celery ribs, thinly sliced
- 2 medium potatoes, peeled and cubed
- 2 cups water
- ½ cup uncooked long grain rice
- 3 tsp. salt
- 1 tsp. pepper

1. In a Dutch oven, cook beef and onions over medium heat until the meat is no longer pink; drain. Add the tomatoes, carrots, celery, potatoes, water, rice, salt and pepper; bring to a boil. Reduce heat; cover and simmer for 30 minutes or until vegetables and rice are tender.

2. Uncover; simmer 20-30 minutes longer or until thickened to desired consistency.

FREEZE OPTION: Freeze cooled stew in freezer containers. To use, partially thaw in refrigerator overnight. Heat through in a saucepan, stirring occasionally and adding a little water if necessary.

1 CUP: 191 cal., 7g fat (3g sat. fat), 35mg chol., 689mg sod., 21g carb. (8g sugars, 2g fiber), 12g pro.

SAVORY BRAISED CHICKEN WITH VEGETABLES

Pick up a fresh baguette to serve with this hearty dish—you'll want it to soak up every last bit of the savory, veggie-laden broth!
—*Michelle Collins, Lake Orion, MI*

PREP: 15 min. • **COOK:** 40 min. • **MAKES:** 6 servings

½ cup seasoned
   bread crumbs
6 boneless skinless
   chicken breast
   halves (4 oz. each)
2 Tbsp. olive oil
1 can (14½ oz.) beef broth
2 Tbsp. tomato paste
1 tsp. poultry seasoning
½ tsp. salt
½ tsp. pepper
1 lb. fresh baby carrots
1 lb. sliced fresh
   mushrooms
2 medium zucchini, sliced
   Sliced French bread
   baguette, optional

1. Place bread crumbs in a shallow bowl. Dip chicken breasts in the bread crumbs to coat both sides; shake off excess.

2. In a Dutch oven, heat oil over medium heat. Add the chicken in batches; cook 2-4 minutes on each side or until browned. Remove the chicken from the pot.

3. Add broth, tomato paste and seasonings to same pot; cook over medium-high heat, stirring to loosen browned bits from pot. Add vegetables and chicken; bring to a boil. Reduce heat; simmer, covered, for 25-30 minutes or until vegetables are tender and a thermometer inserted in chicken reads 165°. If desired, serve with baguette.

1 CHICKEN BREAST HALF WITH 1 CUP VEGETABLE MIXTURE: 247 cal., 8g fat (1g sat. fat), 63mg chol., 703mg sod., 16g carb. (6g sugars, 3g fiber), 28g pro. *Diabetic exchanges:* 3 lean meat, 2 vegetable, 1 fat, ½ starch.

TURKEY DUMPLING STEW

My mom made this stew when I was young, and it was always a hit.
Since it's not too time-consuming, I often make it on weekends for
our children, who love the tender dumplings.
—*Becky Mohr, Appleton, WI*

PREP: 20 min. • **COOK:** 50 min. • **MAKES:** 6 servings

4 bacon strips,
   finely chopped
1½ lbs. turkey breast
   tenderloins, cut
   into 1-in. pieces
4 medium carrots, sliced
2 small onions, quartered
2 celery ribs, sliced
1 bay leaf
¼ tsp. dried rosemary,
   crushed
2 cups water, divided
1 can (14½ oz.)
   reduced-sodium
   chicken broth
3 Tbsp. all-purpose flour
½ tsp. salt
⅛ to ¼ tsp. pepper
1 cup reduced-fat
   biscuit/baking mix
⅓ cup plus 1 Tbsp.
   fat-free milk
   Coarsely ground
   pepper and chopped
   fresh parsley, optional

1. In a Dutch oven, cook bacon over medium heat until crisp, stirring occasionally. Remove with a slotted spoon; drain on paper towels. Reserve 2 tsp. drippings.

2. Adjust heat to medium-high; saute turkey in the drippings until lightly browned. Add vegetables, herbs, 1¾ cups water and broth; bring to a boil. Reduce the heat; simmer, covered, until the vegetables are tender, 20-30 minutes.

3. Mix flour and the remaining water until smooth; stir into the turkey mixture. Bring to a boil; cook and stir until thickened, about 2 minutes. Discard bay leaf. Stir in salt, pepper and bacon.

4. In a small bowl, mix biscuit mix and milk to form a soft dough; drop in 6 mounds on top of simmering stew. Cover; simmer 15 minutes or until a toothpick inserted in dumplings comes out clean. If desired, sprinkle with pepper and parsley before serving.

1 SERVING: 284 cal., 6g fat (1g sat. fat), 52mg chol., 822mg sod., 24g carb. (6g sugars, 2g fiber), 34g pro. *Diabetic exchanges:* 4 lean meat, 1 starch, 1 vegetable, ½ fat.

SLOW-SIMMERED BURGUNDY BEEF STEW

My mother-in-law shared this recipe with me almost 25 years ago. Ever since, it's been a go-to whenever I need a lot of food without a lot of fussing.
—*Mary Lou Timpson, CO City, AZ*

PREP: 30 min. • **BAKE:** 1¾ hours • **MAKES:** 4 servings

1½ lbs. beef stew meat (1¼-in. pieces)
3 Tbsp. all-purpose flour
¾ tsp. salt
2 to 4 tsp. canola oil, divided
2 tsp. beef bouillon granules
2 tsp. dried parsley flakes
1½ tsp. Italian seasoning
2 cups water
1 cup Burgundy wine or beef stock
3 medium potatoes (about 1⅓ lbs.), peeled and quartered
1 cup fresh mushrooms, halved
1 medium onion, cut into 8 wedges
2 medium carrots, cut into 1-in. pieces
2 celery ribs, cut into ½-in. pieces
    Additional water, optional

1. Preheat oven to 350°. Toss beef with flour and salt to coat lightly; shake off excess. In an ovenproof Dutch oven, heat 2 tsp. oil over medium heat. Brown beef in batches, adding additional oil as needed. Remove from pan.

2. Add bouillon, herbs, 2 cups water and wine to same pot; bring to a boil, stirring to loosen browned bits from pot. Add beef; return to a boil. Transfer pot to oven; bake, covered, 1 hour.

3. Stir in vegetables and, if desired, thin with additional water. Bake, covered, until the beef and vegetables are tender, 45-60 minutes.

1½ CUPS: 419 cal., 15g fat (5g sat. fat), 106mg chol., 949mg sod., 33g carb. (5g sugars, 4g fiber), 37g pro.

VEG JAMBALAYA

This vegetarian version of the flavorful entree won't leave you hungry—
it uses convenient canned beans in place of chicken and shrimp for protein.
—*Crystal Jo Bruns, Iliff, CO*

PREP: 10 min. • **COOK:** 30 min. • **MAKES:** 6 servings

1　Tbsp. canola oil
1　medium green
　　pepper, chopped
1　medium onion,
　　chopped
1　celery rib, chopped
3　garlic cloves, minced
2　cups water
1　can (14½ oz.) diced
　　tomatoes, undrained
1　can (8 oz.) tomato sauce
½　tsp. Italian seasoning
¼　tsp. salt
¼　tsp. crushed red
　　pepper flakes
⅛　tsp. fennel seed, crushed
1　cup uncooked long
　　grain rice
1　can (16 oz.) butter
　　beans, rinsed
　　and drained
1　can (16 oz.) red beans,
　　rinsed and drained

1. In a Dutch oven, heat oil over medium-high heat. Add the green pepper, onion and celery; cook and stir until tender. Add garlic; cook 1 minute longer.

2. Add the water, tomatoes, tomato sauce and seasonings. Bring to a boil; stir in rice. Reduce heat; cover and simmer for 15-18 minutes or until liquid is absorbed and rice is tender. Stir in beans; heat through.

1⅓ CUPS: 281 cal., 3g fat (0 sat. fat), 0 chol., 796mg sod., 56g carb. (6g sugars, 9g fiber), 11g pro.

SUNDAY CASSOULET

Wine lends a warm background taste to this take on a traditional French stew. The recipe feeds 10, making it a great option when you're expecting guests — or wanting some leftovers for weekday lunches!
—*Lynn Stein, Joseph, OR*

PREP: 25 min. • **COOK:** 40 min. • **MAKES:** 10 servings (4 qt.)

1 lb. pork tenderloin, cut into ½-in. pieces
1 lb. smoked turkey kielbasa, cut into ½-in. pieces
1 Tbsp. olive oil
3 medium carrots, chopped
1 large onion, cut into wedges
4 garlic cloves, minced
2 cans (14½ oz. each) no-salt-added stewed tomatoes, cut up
1 can (14½ oz.) reduced-sodium chicken broth
3 tsp. herbes de Provence
1½ tsp. garlic powder
1½ tsp. dried basil
½ tsp. dried oregano
¼ tsp. pepper
4 cans (15½ oz. each) great northern beans, rinsed and drained, divided
¾ cup white wine or additional chicken broth, divided

1. In a Dutch oven coated with cooking spray, saute pork and kielbasa in oil until lightly browned; drain. Add carrots and onion; saute 4 minutes longer. Add garlic; cook for 1 minute longer. Stir in the tomatoes, broth and seasonings. Bring to a boil. Reduce heat; cover and simmer for 10 minutes.

2. Place 1 can of beans in a food processor; add ¼ cup wine. Cover and process until pureed. Stir into the meat mixture. Stir in the remaining beans and wine. Bring to a boil. Reduce heat; simmer, uncovered, for 8-10 minutes or until the meat and vegetables are tender.

FREEZE OPTION: Freeze cooled cassoulet in airtight freezer containers. To use, partially thaw in refrigerator overnight. Heat through in a saucepan, stirring occasionally and adding a little broth or water if necessary.

1½ CUPS: 316 cal., 5g fat (1g sat. fat), 41mg chol., 959mg sod., 40g carb. (8g sugars, 11g fiber), 25g pro.

CHICKEN CHILI WITH BLACK BEANS

Because this dish looks different than traditional chili, my family was hesitant to try it at first. Thanks to the full, hearty flavor, it's become a real favorite.
—*Jeanette Urbom, Louisburg, KS*

PREP: 10 min. • **COOK:** 25 min. • **MAKES:** 10 servings (3 qt.)

3 whole boneless skinless chicken breasts (1¾ lbs.), cubed
2 medium sweet red peppers, chopped
1 large onion, chopped
3 Tbsp. olive oil
1 can (4 oz.) chopped green chiles
4 garlic cloves, minced
2 Tbsp. chili powder
2 tsp. ground cumin
1 tsp. ground coriander
2 cans (15 oz. each) black beans, rinsed and drained
1 can (28 oz.) Italian stewed tomatoes, cut up
1 cup chicken broth or beer
½ to 1 cup water

In a Dutch oven, saute the chicken, red peppers and onion in oil until the chicken is no longer pink, about 5 minutes. Add the green chiles, garlic, chili powder, cumin and coriander; cook 1 minute longer. Stir in the beans, tomatoes, broth and ½ cup water; bring to a boil. Reduce heat and simmer, uncovered, for 15 minutes, stirring often and adding more water as necessary.

1¼ CUPS: 236 cal., 6g fat (1g sat. fat), 44mg chol., 561mg sod., 21g carb. (5g sugars, 6g fiber), 22g pro. *Diabetic exchanges:* 2 lean meat, 1½ starch, 1 fat.

CREOLE JAMBALAYA

Red jambalaya is a traditional Louisiana Creole dish with deep roots in French and Spanish cuisines. Tomatoes, seafood, rice, onions, green peppers and celery are the key ingredients in this southern favorite. Most recipes also call for chicken or sausage, but mine uses ham for an easy taste twist.

—Ruby Williams, Bogalusa, LA

PREP: 20 min. • **COOK:** 35 min. • **MAKES:** 8 servings

¾ cup chopped onion
½ cup chopped celery
¼ cup chopped green pepper
2 Tbsp. butter
2 garlic cloves, minced
2 cups cubed fully cooked ham
1 can (28 oz.) diced tomatoes, undrained
1 can (10½ oz.) condensed beef broth, undiluted
1 cup uncooked long grain white rice
1 cup water
1 tsp. sugar
1 tsp. dried thyme
½ tsp. chili powder
¼ tsp. pepper
1½ lbs. fresh or frozen uncooked shrimp, peeled and deveined
1 Tbsp. minced fresh parsley

1. In a Dutch oven over medium-high heat, saute the onion, celery and green pepper in butter until tender. Add garlic; cook 1 minute longer. Add the next 9 ingredients; bring to a boil over medium-high heat. Reduce heat; cover and simmer until rice is tender, about 25 minutes.

2. Add shrimp and parsley; simmer, uncovered, until the shrimp turn pink, 7-10 minutes.

1 CUP: 270 cal., 6g fat (3g sat. fat), 132mg chol., 974mg sod., 29g carb. (5g sugars, 2g fiber), 25g pro.

SAUSAGE & KALE LENTIL STEW

I made a pot of this soup when visiting my sister and her family. Now I bring it along when I stop by, or I pack up a few containers for my nephew, who appreciates a home-cooked meal while he's away at college.
—*Tiffany Ihle, Bronx, NY*

PREP: 20 min. • **COOK:** 45 min. • **MAKES:** 6 servings (2 qt.)

1   lb. bulk pork sausage
10 baby carrots, chopped
    (about ¾ cup)
1   small onion,
    finely chopped
4   garlic cloves, minced
4   plum tomatoes, halved
¾   cup roasted sweet
    red peppers
1   cup dried lentils, rinsed
2   cans (14½ oz. each)
    vegetable broth
1   bay leaf
½   tsp. ground cumin
¼   tsp. pepper
2   cups coarsely chopped
    fresh kale

1. In a Dutch oven, cook sausage, carrots and onion over medium-high heat until sausage is no longer pink, breaking up sausage into crumbles, 8-10 minutes. Stir in garlic; cook 2 minutes longer. Drain.

2. Place the tomatoes and red peppers in a food processor; process until finely chopped. Add to the sausage mixture; stir in lentils, broth and seasonings. Bring to a boil. Reduce heat; simmer, covered, for 20 minutes, stirring occasionally.

3. Stir in kale; cook until the lentils and kale are tender, 10-15 minutes. Remove the bay leaf.

FREEZE OPTION: Freeze cooled stew in freezer containers. To use, partially thaw in refrigerator overnight. Heat through in a saucepan, stirring occasionally.

1⅓ CUPS: 339 cal., 17g fat (5g sat. fat), 41mg chol., 1007mg sod., 29g carb. (5g sugars, 5g fiber), 17g pro.

STOVETOP TARRAGON CHICKEN

My oldest daughter can't get enough of the tarragon sauce that comes with this delicious chicken dish. She uses biscuits to soak up every scrumptious drop. My husband and I like it over mashed potatoes.
— *Tina Westover, La Mesa, CA*

PREP: 10 min. • **COOK:** 30 min. • **MAKES:** 4 servings

4   boneless skinless chicken breast halves (5 oz. each)
2   tsp. paprika
1   Tbsp. olive oil
1   pkg. (10 oz.) julienned carrots
½   lb. sliced fresh mushrooms
2   cans (10¾ oz. each) reduced-fat reduced-sodium condensed cream of chicken soup, undiluted
3   tsp. dried tarragon
1   Tbsp. lemon juice
3   small zucchini, thinly sliced

1. Sprinkle chicken with paprika. In a Dutch oven, heat oil over medium heat. Cook chicken 2 minutes on each side or until lightly browned; remove from pot.

2. Add carrots and mushrooms to same pot; cook, covered, 6-8 minutes or until carrots are crisp-tender, stirring occasionally. In a small bowl, mix the soup, tarragon and lemon juice until blended; pour over the vegetables. Return chicken to pot. Bring to a boil; reduce heat to low. Cook, covered, 8 minutes. Top with zucchini; cook, covered, 6-8 minutes longer or until a thermometer inserted in chicken reads 165° and vegetables are tender.

1 CHICKEN BREAST WITH 1 CUP VEGETABLES:
345 cal., 11g fat (3g sat. fat), 85mg chol., 649mg sod., 28g carb. (16g sugars, 5g fiber), 35g pro. *Diabetic exchanges:* 4 lean meat, 2 vegetable, 1 starch, 1 fat.

**PRESSURE-COOKER
SWEET & SOUR PORK, 150**

SLOW COOKER & INSTANT POT®

Cook it fast or let it simmer for hours—today's favorite kitchen gadgets make dinner convenient and oh, so delicious!

Pressure-Cooker Buffalo Shrimp Mac & Cheese 126
Apple Chicken Stew. 129
Carolina Shrimp & Cheddar Grits 130
Pressure-Cooker Mediterranean Chicken Orzo. 133
Slow-Cooker Spicy Pork Chili 134
Slow-Cooked Beef & Veggies 137
Pressure-Cooker Tuna Noodle Casserole 138
Oktoberfest Pork Roast 141
Slow-Cooked Enchilada Casserole. 142
Slow-Cooker Chicken Bog 145
Pressure-Cooker Cuban Ropa Vieja 146
Creamy Bratwurst Stew 149
Pressure-Cooker Sweet & Sour Pork 150
Pressure-Cooker Italian Shrimp & Pasta 153
Manchester Stew 154
Lora's Pressure-Cooker Red Beans & Rice 157
German Potato Salad with Sausage 158
North African Chicken & Rice 161
Zesty Beef Stew 162
Pressure-Cooker Chicken Tikka Masala 165

PRESSURE-COOKER BUFFALO SHRIMP MAC & CHEESE

Rich, creamy and slightly spicy, this shrimp and pasta dish does it all.
It's a nice new twist on popular Buffalo chicken dishes.
—Robin Haas, Cranston, RI

PREP: 15 min. • **COOK:** 10 min. + releasing • **MAKES:** 6 servings

2 cups 2% milk
1 cup half-and-half cream
1 Tbsp. unsalted butter
1 tsp. ground mustard
½ tsp. onion powder
¼ tsp. white pepper
¼ tsp. ground nutmeg
1½ cups uncooked elbow macaroni
2 cups shredded cheddar cheese
1 cup shredded Gouda or Swiss cheese
¾ lb. frozen cooked salad shrimp, thawed
1 cup crumbled blue cheese
2 Tbsp. Louisiana-style hot sauce
2 Tbsp. minced fresh chives
2 Tbsp. minced fresh parsley
Additional Louisiana-style hot sauce, optional

1. In a 6-qt. electric pressure cooker, combine the first 7 ingredients; stir in macaroni. Lock lid; close pressure-release valve. Adjust to pressure-cook on high for 3 minutes. Allow pressure to naturally release for 4 minutes, then quick-release any remaining pressure. Press cancel.

2. Select the saute setting, and adjust for normal heat. Stir in shredded cheeses, shrimp, blue cheese and hot sauce. Cook until heated through, 5-6 minutes. Just before serving, stir in chives, parsley and, if desired, additional hot sauce.

1 SERVING: 551 cal., 34g fat (20g sat. fat), 228mg chol., 1269mg sod., 22g carb. (7g sugars, 1g fiber), 38g pro.

APPLE CHICKEN STEW

My husband and I enjoy visiting the apple orchards
in nearby Nebraska City. We always make sure to buy
extra cider to use in this sensational slow-cooked stew.
—*Carol Mathias, Lincoln, NE*

PREP: 35 min. • **COOK:** 3 hours • **MAKES:** 8 servings (2 qt.)

1½ tsp. salt
¾ tsp. dried thyme
½ tsp. pepper
¼ to ½ tsp. caraway seeds
1½ lbs. potatoes (about
    4 medium), cut into
    ¾-in. pieces
4 medium carrots, cut
    into ¼-in. slices
1 medium red onion,
    halved and sliced
1 celery rib, thinly sliced
2 lbs. boneless skinless
    chicken breasts, cut
    into 1-in. pieces
2 Tbsp. olive oil
1 bay leaf
1 large tart apple, peeled
    and cut into 1-in. cubes
1 Tbsp. cider vinegar
1¼ cups apple cider or juice
    Minced fresh parsley

1. Mix the first 4 ingredients. In a 5-qt. slow cooker, layer vegetables; sprinkle with half of the salt mixture.

2. Toss chicken with oil and the remaining salt mixture. In a large skillet over medium-high heat, brown the chicken in batches. Add to slow cooker. Top with bay leaf and apple. Add vinegar and cider.

3. Cook, covered, on high until the chicken is no longer pink and vegetables are tender, 3-3½ hours. Discard bay leaf. Stir before serving. Sprinkle with parsley.

1 CUP: 284 cal., 6g fat (1g sat. fat), 63mg chol., 533mg sod., 31g carb. (9g sugars, 4g fiber), 26g pro. *Diabetic exchanges:* 3 lean meat, 2 starch, 1 fat.

CAROLINA SHRIMP & CHEDDAR GRITS

Shrimp and grits are a house favorite, if only we could agree on a recipe! I stirred things up with cheddar and Cajun seasoning to find a winner that everyone in the family loves.
—*Charlotte Price, Raleigh, NC*

PREP: 15 min. • **COOK:** 2¾ hours • **MAKES:** 6 servings

1 cup uncooked stone-ground grits
1 large garlic clove, minced
½ tsp. salt
¼ tsp. pepper
4 cups water
2 cups shredded cheddar cheese
¼ cup butter, cubed
1 lb. peeled and deveined cooked shrimp (31-40 per lb.)
2 medium tomatoes, seeded and finely chopped
4 green onions, finely chopped
2 Tbsp. chopped fresh parsley
4 tsp. lemon juice
2 to 3 tsp. Cajun seasoning

1. Place the first 5 ingredients in a 3-qt. slow cooker; stir to combine. Cook, covered, on high until water is absorbed and grits are tender, 2½-3 hours, stirring every 45 minutes.

2. Stir in cheese and butter until melted. Stir in the remaining ingredients; cook, covered, on high until heated through, 15-30 minutes.

1⅓ CUPS: 417 cal., 22g fat (13g sat. fat), 175mg chol., 788mg sod., 27g carb. (2g sugars, 2g fiber), 27g pro.

PRESSURE-COOKER MEDITERRANEAN CHICKEN ORZO

Orzo pasta with chicken, olives and herbes de Provence has the bright flavors of Mediterranean cuisine. Here's a bonus: Leftovers reheat well.
—*Thomas Faglon, Somerset, NJ*

PREP: 15 min. • **COOK:** 5 min. + standing • **MAKES:** 6 servings

6 boneless skinless chicken thighs (about 1½ lbs.), cut into 1-in. pieces
2 cups reduced-sodium chicken broth
2 medium tomatoes, chopped
1 cup sliced pitted green olives, drained
1 cup sliced pitted ripe olives, drained
1 large carrot, halved lengthwise and chopped
1 small red onion, finely chopped
1 Tbsp. grated lemon zest
3 Tbsp. lemon juice
2 Tbsp. butter
1 Tbsp. herbes de Provence
1 cup uncooked orzo pasta

1. In a 6-qt. electric pressure cooker, combine the first 11 ingredients; stir to combine. Lock lid; close pressure-release valve. Adjust pressure to pressure-cook on high for 8 minutes. Quick-release pressure.

2. Add orzo. Lock lid; close pressure-release valve. Adjust to pressure-cook on low for 3 minutes. Allow pressure to naturally release for 4 minutes, then quick-release any remaining pressure. Let stand 8-10 minutes before serving.

1 SERVING: 415 cal., 19g fat (5g sat. fat), 86mg chol., 941mg sod., 33g carb. (4g sugars, 3g fiber), 27g pro.

SLOW-COOKER SPICY PORK CHILI

Tender pork adds extra heartiness to this slow-cooked chili. You can use pork tenderloin, boneless pork roast or boneless pork chops for the pork called for in the recipe—your choice!
—Taste of Home *Test Kitchen*

PREP: 10 min. • **COOK:** 6 hours • **MAKES:** 6 servings (1½ qt.)

2 lbs. boneless pork, cut into ½-in. cubes
1 Tbsp. canola oil
1 can (28 oz.) crushed tomatoes
2 cups frozen corn
1 can (15 oz.) black beans, rinsed and drained
1 cup chopped onion
2 cups beef broth
1 can (4 oz.) chopped green chiles
1 Tbsp. chili powder
1 tsp. minced garlic
½ tsp. salt
½ tsp. cayenne pepper
½ tsp. pepper
¼ cup minced fresh cilantro
Shredded cheddar cheese, optional

1. In a large skillet, cook pork in oil over medium-high heat until browned, 5-6 minutes. Transfer pork and drippings to a 5-qt. slow cooker. Stir in the tomatoes, corn, beans, onion, broth, chiles, chili powder, garlic, salt, cayenne and pepper.

2. Cover and cook on low until the pork is tender, 6-7 hours. Stir in cilantro. Top individual servings with shredded cheese if desired.

1¾ CUPS: 395 cal., 12g fat (4g sat. fat), 89mg chol., 1055mg sod., 34g carb. (9g sugars, 8g fiber), 39g pro.

SLOW-COOKED BEEF & VEGGIES

My husband and I came up with this soothing slow-cooker recipe when we were looking to cut the fat but still enjoy flavorful meals. This simple and hearty beef dish fits the bill perfectly.
—LaDonna Reed, Ponca City, OK

PREP: 15 min. + marinating • **COOK:** 8 hours • **MAKES:** 2 servings

1 boneless beef top round steak (½ lb.), cut into two pieces
Dash seasoned salt, optional
Dash pepper
Dash garlic powder
1 cup Italian salad dressing
½ cup water
1 Tbsp. browning sauce, optional
2 medium carrots, cut into 2-in. pieces
2 medium red potatoes, cubed
1 small onion, sliced
½ small green pepper, cut into small chunks

1. Sprinkle one side of steak with seasoned salt (if desired) and pepper; sprinkle the other side with garlic powder. Cover and refrigerate for 2-3 hours or overnight.

2. In a 3-qt. slow cooker, combine the salad dressing, water and browning sauce. Add carrots and potatoes; toss to coat. Add steak and coat with sauce. Top with onion and green pepper.

3. Cover and cook on low until meat is tender, 8-9 hours.

1 SERVING: 505 cal., 22g fat (3g sat. fat), 63mg chol., 1283mg sod., 36g carb. (14g sugars, 5g fiber), 29g pro.

PRESSURE-COOKER TUNA NOODLE CASSEROLE

We tweaked this family-friendly classic to work for the pressure cooker. It's easy, wholesome and totally homemade!
—Taste of Home *Test Kitchen*

....

PREP: 25 min. • **COOK:** 15 min. + releasing • **MAKES:** 10 servings

¼ cup butter, cubed
½ lb. sliced fresh mushrooms
1 medium onion, chopped
1 medium sweet pepper, chopped
1 tsp. salt, divided
1 tsp. pepper, divided
2 garlic cloves, minced
¼ cup all-purpose flour
2 cups reduced-sodium chicken broth
2 cups half-and-half cream
4 cups (8 oz.) uncooked egg noodles
3 cans (5 oz. each) light tuna in water
2 Tbsp. lemon juice
2 cups shredded Monterey Jack cheese
2 cups frozen peas, thawed
2 cups crushed potato chips

1. Select saute setting on a 6-qt. electric pressure cooker and adjust for high heat. Add butter. When melted, add mushrooms, onion, sweet pepper, ½ tsp. salt and ½ tsp. pepper; cook and stir until tender, 6-8 minutes. Add garlic; cook 1 minute longer. Stir in flour until blended. Gradually whisk in broth. Bring to a boil, stirring constantly; cook and stir until thickened, 1-2 minutes. Stir in cream and noodles. Lock lid; close pressure-release valve. Adjust to pressure-cook on high for 3 minutes. Allow pressure to naturally release for 3 minutes, then quick-release any remaining pressure. Press cancel.

2. Meanwhile, in a small bowl, combine tuna, lemon juice and remaining salt and pepper. Select saute setting, and adjust for low heat. Stir cheese, tuna mixture and peas into noodle mixture. Cook until heated through. Just before serving, sprinkle with potato chips.

1 SERVING: 393 cal., 21g fat (12g sat. fat), 84mg chol., 752mg sod., 28g carb. (5g sugars, 3g fiber), 22g pro.

OKTOBERFEST PORK ROAST

My mom used to make a version of this roast when
I was growing up. It has all of our favorite fall flavors,
such as apples, pork roast, sauerkraut and potatoes.
—*Tonya Swain, Seville, OH*

PREP: 35 min. • **COOK:** 8 hours • **MAKES:** 8 servings

16 small red potatoes
1   can (14 oz.) sauerkraut,
    rinsed and well drained
2   large tart apples, peeled
    and cut into wedges
1   lb. smoked kielbasa
    or Polish sausage, cut
    into 16 slices
2   Tbsp. brown sugar
1   tsp. caraway seeds
1   tsp. salt, divided
1   tsp. pepper, divided
1   boneless pork loin roast
    (3 lbs.)
3   Tbsp. canola oil

1. Place potatoes in a greased 6-qt. slow cooker. Top with sauerkraut, apples and kielbasa. Sprinkle with brown sugar, caraway seeds, ½ tsp. salt and ½ tsp. pepper.

2. Cut roast in half; sprinkle with the remaining salt and pepper. In a large skillet, brown meat in oil on all sides. Transfer to slow cooker.

3. Cover and cook on low until the meat and vegetables are tender, 8-10 hours. Skim fat and thicken cooking liquid if desired.

1 SERVING: 562 cal., 29g fat (9g sat. fat), 123mg chol., 1290mg sod., 31g carb. (10g sugars, 4g fiber), 43g pro.

✳ TEST KITCHEN TIP

An easy way to thicken your cooking liquid is to make a slurry paste of 1 Tbsp. cornstarch to 1 Tbsp. water— then stir the paste into the cooking liquid and let it cook for 2 minutes over medium heat.

SLOW-COOKED ENCHILADA CASSEROLE

Tortilla chips and a side salad turn this casserole into
a fun and festive meal with very little effort.
—*Denise Waller, Omaha, NE*

PREP: 20 min. • **COOK:** 6 hours • **MAKES:** 6 servings

1 lb. ground beef
2 cans (10 oz. each)
   enchilada sauce
1 can (10¾ oz.)
   condensed cream of
   onion soup, undiluted
¼ tsp. salt
1 pkg. (8½ oz.) flour
   tortillas, torn
3 cups shredded
   cheddar cheese

1. In a skillet, cook beef over medium heat until no longer pink; drain. Stir in enchilada sauce, soup and salt.

2. In a 3-qt. slow cooker, layer a third of the beef mixture, tortillas and cheese. Repeat the layers twice. Cover and cook on low until heated through, 6-8 hours.

1 SERVING: 568 cal., 35g fat (16g sat. fat), 105mg chol., 1610mg sod., 30g carb. (4g sugars, 3g fiber), 31g pro.

SLOW-COOKER CHICKEN BOG

Chicken Bog is a South Carolina tradition with lots of variations,
but the core ingredients remain: sausage, chicken and rice.
This slow-cooked rendition is a simple take on the classic.
—*Anna Hanson, Spanish Fork, UT*

PREP: 20 min. • **COOK:** 4 hours • **MAKES:** 6 servings

1 Tbsp. canola oil
1 medium onion,
  chopped
8 oz. smoked sausage,
  halved and sliced
  ½ in. thick
3 garlic cloves, minced
5 cups chicken broth,
  divided
2 cups uncooked
  converted rice
1 tsp. salt
1 tsp. pepper
1 rotisserie chicken (about
  3 lbs.), meat removed
  and shredded
  Thinly sliced green
  onions, optional
  Hot sauce

1. In a large skillet, heat oil over medium heat. Add onion and sausage; cook until sausage is lightly browned. Add garlic and cook 1 minute longer; transfer to a 5-qt. slow cooker.

2. Stir in 4 cups broth, rice, salt and pepper. Cook, covered, on low until the rice is tender, 4-5 hours. Stir in chicken and the remaining broth. Cook, covered, on low until the chicken is heated through, about 30 minutes. If desired, sprinkle with green onions. Serve with hot sauce.

FREEZE OPTION: Omit green onions and hot sauce; freeze cooled meat mixture, juices and rice in freezer containers. To use, partially thaw in refrigerator overnight. Microwave, covered, on high until heated through, stirring gently; add a little broth or water if necessary.

1⅓ CUPS: 681 cal., 30g fat (9g sat. fat), 134mg chol., 1728mg sod., 54g carb. (3g sugars, 0 fiber), 45g pro.

PRESSURE-COOKER CUBAN ROPA VIEJA

This recipe offers a great authentic Cuban taste that can be prepared at home. I love having this as a go-to recipe for a weeknight meal.
—*Melissa Pelkey Hass, Waleska, GA*

PREP: 25 min. • **COOK:** 20 min. + releasing • **MAKES:** 8 servings

6   bacon strips, chopped
2   beef flank steak (1 lb. each), cut in half
1   can (28 oz.) crushed tomatoes
2   cups beef stock
1   can (6 oz.) tomato paste
5   garlic cloves, minced
1   Tbsp. ground cumin
2   tsp. dried thyme
¾   tsp. salt
½   tsp. pepper
1   medium onion, thinly sliced
1   medium sweet pepper, sliced
1   medium green pepper, sliced
¼   cup minced fresh cilantro
    Hot cooked rice

1. Select saute setting on a 6-qt. electric pressure cooker and adjust for high heat; add bacon. Cook bacon until crisp, stirring occasionally. Remove with a slotted spoon; drain on paper towels.

2. In the drippings, brown steak in batches. Return bacon to the pressure cooker. In a large bowl, combine tomatoes, beef stock, tomato paste, garlic, seasonings, onions and peppers; pour over the meat. Lock lid; close pressure-release valve. Adjust to pressure-cook on high for 12 minutes. Allow pressure to naturally release for 10 minutes, then quick-release any remaining pressure.

3. Shred beef with 2 forks; return to the pressure cooker. Stir in cilantro. Remove with a slotted spoon; serve with rice.

1 SERVING: 335 cal., 17g fat (6g sat. fat), 68mg chol., 765mg sod., 17g carb. (9g sugars, 4g fiber), 29g pro.

CREAMY BRATWURST STEW

I adapted a baked stew recipe from the newspaper to create
a simple slow-cooked version. Rich, hearty and creamy,
it is the best comfort food for cold winter nights.
—*Susan Holmes, Germantown, WI*

PREP: 20 min. • **COOK:** 6½ hours • **MAKES:** 8 servings (2 qt.)

1¾ lbs. potatoes (about
    4 medium), peeled
    and cubed
2 medium carrots,
    chopped
2 celery ribs, chopped
1 medium onion,
    chopped
1 medium green
    pepper, chopped
2 lbs. uncooked
    bratwurst links
½ cup chicken broth
1 tsp. salt
1 tsp. dried basil
½ tsp. pepper
2 cups half-and-half
    cream
1 Tbsp. cornstarch
3 Tbsp. cold water

1. Place the first 5 ingredients in a 5-qt. slow cooker; toss to combine. Top with bratwurst. Mix broth and seasonings; pour over top.

2. Cook, covered, on low until the sausage is cooked through and the vegetables are tender, 6-7 hours. Remove the sausages from slow cooker; cut into 1-in. slices. Return sausages to potato mixture; stir in cream.

3. Mix cornstarch and water until smooth; stir into stew. Cook, covered, on high until thickened, about 30 minutes.

1 CUP: 544 cal., 39g fat (15g sat. fat), 114mg chol., 1367mg sod., 25g carb. (5g sugars, 2g fiber), 19g pro.

PRESSURE-COOKER SWEET & SOUR PORK

Even though a co-worker gave me this recipe more than 20 years ago, my family still enjoys it today. This updated version for an electric pressure cooker makes it all the more convenient.
—*Martha Nickerson, Hancock, ME*

PREP: 20 min. • **COOK:** 15 min. • **MAKES:** 6 servings

2 Tbsp. plus
   1½ tsp. paprika
1½ lbs. boneless pork loin
   roast, cut into 1-in. strips
1 Tbsp. canola oil
1 can (20 oz.)
   unsweetened
   pineapple chunks
1 medium onion,
   chopped
1 medium green
   pepper, chopped
¼ cup cider vinegar
3 Tbsp. packed
   brown sugar
3 Tbsp. reduced-sodium
   soy sauce
1 Tbsp. Worcestershire
   sauce
½ tsp. salt
2 Tbsp. cornstarch
¼ cup cold water
   Thinly sliced/chopped
   green onions, optional
   Hot cooked rice,
   optional

1. Place paprika in a large shallow dish. Add pork, a few pieces at a time, and turn to coat. Select saute setting on a 6-qt. electric pressure cooker and adjust for medium heat; add oil. Brown the pork in batches. Return all pork to the pressure cooker.

2. Drain pineapple, reserving the juice; refrigerate pineapple. Add pineapple juice, onion, green pepper, vinegar, brown sugar, soy sauce, Worcestershire sauce and salt to the pressure cooker. Lock lid; close pressure-release valve. Adjust to pressure-cook on high for 10 minutes. Quick-release pressure.

3. Select saute setting and adjust for high heat; bring liquid to a boil. In a small bowl, mix cornstarch and water until smooth; gradually stir into pork mixture. Add pineapple. Cook and stir until sauce is thickened, 1-2 minutes. If desired, sprinkle with green onions and serve over rice.

1 SERVING: 312 cal., 10g fat (3g sat. fat), 73mg chol., 592mg sod., 28g carb. (21g sugars, 2g fiber), 27g pro.

PRESSURE-COOKER ITALIAN SHRIMP & PASTA

This dish will remind you a bit of classic shrimp Creole, but it has a surprise Italian twist. Pressure-cooking gives it hands-off ease — perfect for company.
—*Karen Edwards, Sanford, ME*

PREP: 20 min. • **COOK:** 20 min. • **MAKES:** 6 servings

2 Tbsp. canola oil
4 boneless skinless chicken thighs (about 1 lb.), cut into 2x1-in. strips
1 can (28 oz.) crushed tomatoes
1½ cups water
2 celery ribs, chopped
1 medium green pepper, cut into 1-in. pieces
1 medium onion, coarsely chopped
2 garlic cloves, minced
1 Tbsp. sugar
½ tsp. salt
½ tsp. Italian seasoning
⅛ to ¼ tsp. cayenne pepper
1 bay leaf
1 cup uncooked orzo or other small pasta
1 lb. peeled and deveined cooked shrimp (31-40 per lb.)

1. Select saute setting on a 6-qt. electric pressure cooker and adjust for high heat. Add 1 Tbsp. oil. When hot, brown chicken in batches, adding oil as needed. Stir in the next 11 ingredients. Lock lid; close pressure-release valve. Adjust to pressure-cook on high for 8 minutes. Quick-release pressure.

2. Discard bay leaf. Select saute setting, and adjust for high heat. Stir in orzo. Cook until al dente, stirring often. Stir in shrimp; cook until the shrimp are heated through, about 2 minutes longer.

1 SERVING: 418 cal., 12g fat (2g sat. fat), 165mg chol., 611mg sod., 40g carb. (10g sugars, 4g fiber), 36g pro. *Diabetic exchanges:* 4 lean meat, 2 starch, 2 vegetable, 1 fat.

MANCHESTER STEW

When studying abroad in England, I was pleasantly surprised at how delicious and diverse vegetarian food in Britain could be. Back in the States, I created this version of my favorite meal from my favorite restaurant. As the enticing aroma fills the kitchen, I'm reminded of my time in England!
—*Kimberly Hammond, Kingwood, TX*

PREP: 25 min. • **COOK:** 8 hours • **MAKES:** 6 servings (2½ qt.)

2 Tbsp. olive oil
2 medium onions, chopped
2 garlic cloves, minced
1 tsp. dried oregano
1 cup dry red wine
1 lb. small red potatoes, quartered
1 can (16 oz.) kidney beans, rinsed and drained
½ lb. sliced fresh mushrooms
2 medium leeks (white portion only), sliced
1 cup fresh baby carrots
2½ cups water
1 can (14½ oz.) no-salt-added diced tomatoes
1 tsp. dried thyme
½ tsp. salt
¼ tsp. pepper
Fresh basil leaves

1. In a large skillet, heat oil over medium-high heat. Add onions; cook and stir until tender, 2-3 minutes. Add garlic and oregano; cook and stir 1 minute longer. Stir in wine. Bring to a boil; cook until the liquid is reduced by half, 3-4 minutes.

2. Transfer to a 5- or 6-qt. slow cooker. Add potatoes, beans, mushrooms, leeks and carrots. Stir in water, tomatoes, thyme, salt and pepper. Cook, covered, on low until the potatoes are tender, 8-10 hours. Top with basil.

1⅔ CUPS: 221 cal., 5g fat (1g sat. fat), 0 chol., 354mg sod., 38g carb. (8g sugars, 8g fiber), 8g pro. *Diabetic exchanges:* 2 starch, 1 vegetable, 1 fat.

LORA'S PRESSURE-COOKER RED BEANS & RICE

My dear mother-in-law gave me this simple recipe—and I've relied on it for years. With meats, beans and savory veggies, it's tasty, balanced and economical, too!
—*Carol Simms, Madison, MS*

PREP: 15 min. + soaking • **COOK:** 30 min. • **MAKES:** 10 servings

1 pkg. (16 oz.) dried kidney beans (about 2½ cups)
2 cups cubed fully cooked ham (about 1 lb.)
1 pkg. (12 oz.) fully cooked andouille chicken sausage links or flavor of choice, sliced
1 medium green pepper, chopped
1 medium onion, chopped
2 celery ribs, chopped
1 Tbsp. hot pepper sauce
2 garlic cloves, minced
1 tsp. salt
Hot cooked rice

1. Rinse and sort beans. Soak overnight according to package directions. Drain, discarding water; rinse with cool water.

2. In a 6-qt. electric pressure cooker, combine beans, ham, sausage, vegetables, pepper sauce, garlic, salt and enough water to cover (about 4 cups). Lock lid; close pressure-release valve. Adjust to pressure-cook on high for 30 minutes. Quick-release pressure. Serve with rice.

1 CUP BEAN MIXTURE: 249 cal., 5g fat (1g sat. fat), 43mg chol., 788mg sod., 31g carb. (2g sugars, 7g fiber), 23g pro. *Diabetic exchanges:* 2 starch, 1 lean meat.

✳ TEST KITCHEN TIP

Use smoked turkey sausage in place of andouille if you prefer a milder dish.

GERMAN POTATO SALAD WITH SAUSAGE

Hearty and saucy, this potato salad is an old family recipe that was updated using cream of potato soup to ease preparation. The sausage and sauerkraut give it a special zip.

— Teresa McGill, Trotwood, OH

PREP: 30 min. • **COOK:** 6 hours • **MAKES:** 5 servings

8 bacon strips, finely chopped
1 large onion, chopped
1 lb. smoked kielbasa or Polish sausage, halved and cut into ½-in. slices
2 lbs. medium red potatoes, cut into chunks
1 can (10¾ oz.) condensed cream of potato soup, undiluted
1 cup sauerkraut, rinsed and well drained
½ cup water
¼ cup cider vinegar
1 Tbsp. sugar
½ tsp. salt
½ tsp. coarsely ground pepper

1. In a large skillet, cook bacon over medium heat until crisp. Remove to paper towels with a slotted spoon to drain. Saute onion in the drippings for 1 minute. Add sausage; cook until lightly browned. Add potatoes; cook 2 minutes longer. Drain.

2. Transfer the sausage mixture to a 3-qt. slow cooker. In a small bowl, combine the soup, sauerkraut, water, vinegar, sugar, salt and pepper. Pour over the sausage mixture. Sprinkle with bacon. Cover and cook on low until the potatoes are tender, 6-7 hours.

1⅔ CUPS: 674 cal., 44g fat (15g sat. fat), 92mg chol., 1643mg sod., 46g carb. (9g sugars, 5g fiber), 22g pro.

NORTH AFRICAN CHICKEN & RICE

I'm always looking to try recipes from different cultures and this dish is a huge favorite with us. We love the spice combinations. This cooks equally well in a slow cooker or pressure cooker.
—*Courtney Stultz, Weir, KS*

PREP: 10 min. • **COOK:** 4 hours • **MAKES:** 8 servings

1 medium onion, diced
1 Tbsp. olive oil
8 boneless skinless chicken thighs (about 2 lbs.)
1 Tbsp. minced fresh cilantro
1 tsp. ground turmeric
1 tsp. paprika
1 tsp. sea salt
½ tsp. pepper
½ tsp. ground cinnamon
½ tsp. chili powder
1 cup golden raisins
½ to 1 cup chopped pitted green olives
1 medium lemon, sliced
2 garlic cloves, minced
½ cup chicken broth or water
4 cups hot cooked brown rice

In a 3- or 4-qt. slow cooker, combine onion and oil. Place chicken thighs on top of onion; sprinkle with the next 7 ingredients. Top with the raisins, olives, lemon and garlic. Add broth. Cook, covered, on low until the chicken is tender, 4-5 hours. Serve with hot cooked rice.

1 SERVING: 386 cal., 13g fat (3g sat. fat), 76mg chol., 556mg sod., 44g carb. (12g sugars, 3g fiber), 25g pro.

✳ TEST KITCHEN TIP

Heavily spiced with a mixture of interesting ingredients, the cuisine from North Africa may be a bit unfamiliar, but you'll fall in love with the new flavor combinations. If olives aren't your favorite, don't leave them out entirely but go with ½ cup. They add a nice underlying flavor as well as a little saltiness to the dish.

ZESTY BEEF STEW

Preparation couldn't be simpler for this hearty stew. I created the dish when I didn't have some of my usual ingredients for vegetable beef soup. My husband said it was the best I'd ever made!

—*Margaret Turza, South Bend, IN*

PREP: 10 min. • **COOK:** 3½ hours • **MAKES:** 6 servings (1½ qt.)

1 lb. beef stew meat, cut into 1-in. cubes

1 pkg. (16 oz.) frozen mixed vegetables, thawed

1 can (15 oz.) pinto beans, rinsed and drained

1½ cups water

1 can (8 oz.) pizza sauce

2 Tbsp. medium pearl barley

1 Tbsp. dried minced onion

2 tsp. beef bouillon granules

¼ tsp. crushed red pepper flakes

In a 3-qt. slow cooker, combine all the ingredients. Cover and cook on low until the meat is tender, 3½-4½ hours.

1 CUP: 251 cal., 6g fat (2g sat. fat), 47mg chol., 526mg sod., 28g carb. (5g sugars, 8g fiber), 21g pro. *Diabetic exchanges:* 3 lean meat, 2 starch.

PRESSURE-COOKER CHICKEN TIKKA MASALA

The flavors of this Indian-style entree keep me coming back for more.
The dish isn't fancy, and it's simply spiced—but it's simply amazing.
—Jaclyn Bell, Logan, UT

PREP: 20 min. • **COOK:** 20 min. • **MAKES:** 8 servings

2 Tbsp. olive oil
½ large onion, finely chopped
4½ tsp. minced fresh gingerroot
4 garlic cloves, minced
1 Tbsp. garam masala
2½ tsp. salt
1½ tsp. ground cumin
1 tsp. paprika
¾ tsp. pepper
½ tsp. cayenne pepper
¼ tsp. ground cinnamon
2½ lbs. boneless skinless chicken breasts, cut into 1½-in. cubes
1 can (29 oz.) tomato puree
⅓ cup water
1 jalapeno pepper, halved and seeded
1 bay leaf
1 Tbsp. cornstarch
1½ cups (12 oz.) plain yogurt
Hot cooked basmati rice
Chopped fresh cilantro, optional

1. Select saute setting on a 6-qt. electric pressure cooker and adjust for medium heat; add oil. Cook onion until tender. Add ginger and garlic; cook 1 minute. Stir in seasonings; cook 30 seconds. Add chicken, tomato puree, water, jalapeno and bay leaf.

2. Lock lid; close pressure-release valve. Adjust to pressure-cook on high for 10 minutes. Quick-release pressure. Discard bay leaf.

3. Select saute setting and adjust for medium heat; bring mixture to a boil. In a small bowl, mix cornstarch and yogurt until smooth; gradually stir into sauce. Cook and stir until sauce is thickened, about 3 minutes. Serve with rice. If desired, sprinkle with cilantro.

1 CUP CHICKEN MIXTURE: 279 cal., 8g fat (2g sat. fat), 84mg chol., 856mg sod., 13g carb. (5g sugars, 2g fiber), 32g pro. *Diabetic exchanges:* 4 lean meat, 1 starch, 1 fat.

✳ DID YOU KNOW?

Tikka masala recipes vary from family to family in Indian culture. Traditionally, chicken is marinated in the yogurt and spice mixture and cooked in a tandoori oven.

TURKEY & SPINACH STUFFING CASSEROLE, 207

CHAPTER 5

CASSEROLES

A convenient dish fresh from the oven, filled with an enticing blend of flavors…Is a casserole the perfect food? It might just be!

Pork & Green Chile Casserole 168

Spinach & Chicken Phyllo Pie 171

Finnish Meat Pie 172

Cranberry Chicken & Wild Rice 175

Reuben Bread Pudding 176

New England Lamb Bake 179

Crescent Turkey Casserole 180

Chicken & Swiss Stuffing Bake 183

Sausage-Stuffed Acorn Squash 184

Chicken Cordon Bleu Bake 187

Beef & Bulgur-Stuffed Zucchini Boats 188

Chicken & Dumpling Casserole 191

Beef & Tater Bake 192

Corn Dog Casserole 195

Cashew Chicken Casserole 196

Broccoli Beef Supper 199

Baked Nectarine Chicken Salad 200

Sweet Potato Enchilada Stack 203

Ham & Veggie Casserole 204

Turkey & Spinach Stuffing Casserole 207

PORK & GREEN CHILE CASSEROLE

I work full time at a local hospital and also part time for some area doctors, so I'm always on the lookout for good, quick recipes to fix for my family. Some of my co-workers and I often exchange recipes. This zippy casserole is one that was brought to a picnic at my house. People raved about it.

—Dianne Esposite, New Middletown, OH

PREP: 20 min. • **BAKE:** 30 min. • **MAKES:** 6 servings

1½ lbs. boneless pork, cut into ½-in. cubes
1 Tbsp. canola oil
1 can (15 oz.) black beans, rinsed and drained
1 can (10¾ oz.) condensed cream of chicken soup, undiluted
1 can (14½ oz.) diced tomatoes, undrained
2 cans (4 oz. each) chopped green chiles
1 cup quick-cooking brown rice
¼ cup water
2 to 3 Tbsp. salsa
1 tsp. ground cumin
½ cup shredded cheddar cheese
Sliced jalapeno pepper, optional

1. Preheat oven to 350°. In a large skillet, brown pork in oil; drain. Stir in the beans, soup, tomatoes, chiles, rice, water, salsa and cumin.

2. Pour into an ungreased 2-qt. baking dish. Bake, uncovered, until bubbly, about 30 minutes. Sprinkle with cheese; let stand for 5 minutes before serving. If desired, serve with jalapeno slices.

FREEZE OPTION: Sprinkle cheese over cooled unbaked casserole. Cover and freeze. To use, partially thaw in refrigerator overnight. Remove from refrigerator 30 minutes before baking. Bake casserole as directed, increasing time as necessary to heat through and for a thermometer inserted in center to read 165°. If desired, serve with jalapeno slices.

1 SERVING: 390 cal., 15g fat (6g sat. fat), 81mg chol., 814mg sod., 29g carb. (3g sugars, 6g fiber), 32g pro.

SPINACH & CHICKEN PHYLLO PIE

For a brunch showstopper, we make chicken pie with phyllo and spinach.
Even our kids go for it. It's so good served with a minty fruit salad.
—*Katie Ferrier, Houston, TX*

PREP: 35 min. • **BAKE:** 35 min. • **MAKES:** 8 servings

2 lbs. ground chicken
1 large onion, chopped
1 tsp. pepper
1 tsp. dried oregano
¾ tsp. salt
½ tsp. ground nutmeg
¼ tsp. crushed red
   pepper flakes
3 pkg. (10 oz. each)
   frozen chopped
   spinach, thawed
   and squeezed dry
4 large eggs,
   lightly beaten
3 cups crumbled
   feta cheese
20 sheets phyllo dough
   (14x9-in. size)
   Cooking spray

1. Preheat oven to 375°. In a large skillet, cook chicken and onion over medium-high heat for 7-9 minutes or until the chicken is no longer pink, breaking up the meat into crumbles; drain. Stir in seasonings. Add spinach; cook and stir until the liquid is evaporated. Transfer to a large bowl; cool slightly. Stir in beaten eggs and cheese.

2. Layer 10 sheets of phyllo dough in a greased 13x9-in. baking dish, spritzing each with cooking spray. (Keep the remaining phyllo covered with a damp towel to prevent it from drying out.) Spread spinach mixture over the phyllo. Top with remaining sheets of phyllo, spritzing each with cooking spray. Cut into 8 rectangles.

3. Bake, uncovered, 35-40 minutes or until golden brown. If necessary, recut rectangles before serving.

1 PIECE: 442 cal., 23g fat (8g sat. fat), 191mg chol., 921mg sod., 25g carb. (3g sugars, 6g fiber), 35g pro.

FINNISH MEAT PIE

We enjoy this hearty, traditional meat pie year-round, but especially during hunting season, when it's good to have a savory, satisfying meal waiting at home. This is one recipe I'll be sure to pass on to our children.
—*Laurel Skoog, Frazee, MN*

PREP: 25 min. + chilling • **BAKE:** 1¼ hours • **MAKES:** 8 servings

1 cup shortening
1 cup boiling water
3 cups all-purpose flour
1 tsp. salt
FILLING
4 cups shredded peeled potatoes
1½ lbs. lean ground beef (90% lean)
2 cups shredded carrots
1 medium onion, chopped
½ cup shredded peeled rutabaga
1½ tsp. salt
¼ tsp. pepper
EGG WASH
1 large egg
1 Tbsp. 2% milk

1. Place shortening in a large bowl. Add boiling water; stir until shortening is melted. In a small bowl, mix flour and salt. Add to the shortening mixture; stir until a soft ball forms. Cover and refrigerate until cooled, about 1 hour.

2. Preheat oven to 350°. Divide dough in half. On a lightly floured surface, roll 1 dough portion into a 17x13-in. rectangle. Transfer to an ungreased 13x9-in. baking dish. Press onto bottom and up the sides of dish. Trim pastry to ½ in. beyond rim of dish.

3. In a large bowl, combine the filling ingredients. Spoon into pastry. Roll out the remaining dough into a 13x9-in. rectangle. Place over filling. Fold bottom pastry over top pastry; press with a fork to seal. In a small bowl, whisk egg and milk; brush over pastry. Cut slits in top. Bake 1¼ hours or until golden brown.

1 SERVING: 610 cal., 31g fat (9g sat. fat), 52mg chol., 790mg sod., 57g carb. (5g sugars, 4g fiber), 23g pro.

✳ TEST KITCHEN TIP

To divide the dough, place on a floured surface and flatten slightly. Cut with a sharp knife, pizza cutter or dough cutter. It's important not to tear the dough, so don't use a serrated knife.

CRANBERRY CHICKEN & WILD RICE

This tender chicken in a sweet-tart cranberry sauce is delicious, and it's so easy to prepare. I love that I can do other things while it bakes.
—*Evelyn Lewis, Independence, MO*

PREP: 10 min. • **BAKE:** 35 min. • **MAKES:** 6 servings

6 boneless skinless chicken breast halves (4 oz. each)
1½ cups hot water
1 pkg. (6.2 oz.) fast-cooking long grain and wild rice mix
1 can (14 oz.) whole-berry cranberry sauce
1 Tbsp. lemon juice
1 Tbsp. reduced-sodium soy sauce
1 Tbsp. Worcestershire sauce

1. Preheat oven to 350°. Place chicken in a 13x9-in. baking dish coated with cooking spray. In a bowl, mix hot water, rice mix and the contents of the seasoning packet; pour around the chicken.

2. In a small bowl, mix the remaining ingredients; pour over the chicken. Bake, covered, until a thermometer inserted in chicken reads 165°, 35-45 minutes.

1 CHICKEN BREAST HALF WITH ½ CUP RICE MIXTURE: 332 cal., 3g fat (1g sat. fat), 63mg chol., 592mg sod., 50g carb. (19g sugars, 2g fiber), 26g pro.

REUBEN BREAD PUDDING

Our Aunt Renee always brought this casserole to family picnics in Chicago. It became so popular that she started bringing two or three. I sometimes use dark rye bread or marbled rye and ham instead of corned beef.

—*Johnna Johnson, Scottsdale, AZ*

PREP: 20 min. • **BAKE:** 35 min. • **MAKES:** 6 servings

4   cups cubed rye bread (about 6 slices)
2   Tbsp. butter, melted
2   cups cubed or shredded cooked corned beef (about ½ lb.)
1   can (14 oz.) sauerkraut, rinsed and well drained
1   cup shredded Swiss cheese, divided
3   large eggs
1   cup 2% milk
⅓   cup prepared Thousand Island salad dressing
1½ tsp. prepared mustard
¼   tsp. pepper

1. Preheat oven to 350°. In a large bowl, toss bread cubes with butter. Stir in corned beef, sauerkraut and ½ cup of the cheese; transfer to a greased 11x7-in. baking dish.

2. In the same bowl, whisk eggs, milk, salad dressing, mustard and pepper; pour over top. Bake, uncovered, 30 minutes. Sprinkle with the remaining cheese. Bake until golden and a knife inserted in the center comes out clean, 5-7 minutes longer.

1 PIECE: 390 cal., 25g fat (10g sat. fat), 165mg chol., 1295mg sod., 21g carb. (7g sugars, 3g fiber), 19g pro.

NEW ENGLAND LAMB BAKE

This dish is hearty and perfect for warming up on a chilly winter evening. The aroma is almost as delightful as the dish itself.

—*Frank Grady, Fort Kent, ME*

PREP: 25 min. • **BAKE:** 1½ hours • **MAKES:** 8 servings

1 Tbsp. canola oil
2 lbs. boneless leg of lamb, cut into 1-in. cubes
1 large onion, chopped
¼ cup all-purpose flour
3 cups chicken broth
2 large leeks (white portion only), cut into ½-in. slices
2 large carrots, sliced
2 Tbsp. minced fresh parsley, divided
½ tsp. dried rosemary, crushed
½ tsp. salt
¼ tsp. pepper
¼ tsp. dried thyme
3 large potatoes, peeled and sliced
3 Tbsp. butter, melted and divided

1. Preheat oven to 375°. In a Dutch oven, heat oil over medium heat. Add lamb and onion; cook and stir until the meat is no longer pink. Stir in flour until blended. Gradually add broth. Bring to a boil; cook until thickened, 1-2 minutes, stirring to loosen browned bits from pan. Add leeks, carrots, 1 Tbsp. parsley, rosemary, salt, pepper and thyme.

2. Spoon into a greased 13x9-in. or 3-qt. baking dish. Cover with potato slices; brush with 2 Tbsp. melted butter. Bake 1 hour; brush potatoes with the remaining butter. Return to oven; bake until meat is tender and potatoes are golden, 30 minutes to 1 hour more. Cool briefly; sprinkle with remaining parsley.

FREEZE OPTION: After baking, let cool completely. Before adding the remaining parsley, cover dish and freeze. Freeze parsley separately. To use, partially thaw casserole in refrigerator overnight. Remove from refrigerator 30 minutes before baking; thaw remaining parsley. Preheat oven to 350°. Reheat, covered, until a thermometer reads 165°, about 1 hour. Sprinkle with remaining parsley.

1 PIECE: 356 cal., 13g fat (5g sat. fat), 82mg chol., 631mg sod., 34g carb. (4g sugars, 4g fiber), 25g pro. *Diabetic exchanges:* 3 starch, 3 lean meat, 1½ fat.

CRESCENT TURKEY CASSEROLE

How do you make a dinner of turkey and vegetables appealing to kids? You turn it into a pie, of course! My version tastes classic, but won't take any time at all.
—Daniela Essman, Perham, MN

TAKES: 30 min. • **MAKES:** 4 servings

½ cup mayonnaise
2 Tbsp. all-purpose flour
1 tsp. chicken bouillon granules
⅛ tsp. pepper
¾ cup 2% milk
2 cups frozen mixed vegetables (about 10 oz.), thawed
1½ cups cubed cooked turkey breast
1 tube (4 oz.) refrigerated crescent rolls

1. Preheat oven to 375°. In a saucepan, mix the first 4 ingredients until smooth; gradually stir in the milk. Bring to a boil over medium heat; cook and stir until thickened, about 2 minutes. Add vegetables and turkey; cook and stir until heated through. Transfer to a greased 8-in. square baking pan.

2. Unroll crescent dough and separate into 8 triangles; arrange over turkey mixture. Bake until casserole is heated through and the topping is golden brown, 15-20 minutes.

1 SERVING: 453 cal., 28g fat (6g sat. fat), 48mg chol., 671mg sod., 26g carb. (7g sugars, 3g fiber), 22g pro.

TURKEY BISCUIT POTPIE: Thaw vegetables; combine with turkey, one 10¾-oz. can condensed cream of chicken soup and ¼ tsp. dried thyme. Place in a deep-dish 9-in. pie plate. Mix 1 cup biscuit/baking mix, ½ cup milk and 1 large egg; spoon over top. Bake at 400° for 25-30 minutes.

TURKEY ASPARAGUS CASSEROLE: Thaw a 10-oz. package of frozen asparagus; combine with turkey, one 10¾-oz. can condensed cream of chicken soup and ¼ cup water. Bake at 350° for 30 minutes; top with a 2.8-oz. can of french-fried onions during last 5 minutes.

CHICKEN & SWISS STUFFING BAKE

I love to cook but just don't have much time. This casserole is both comforting and fast, which makes it my favorite kind of recipe. I serve it with a green salad.
—*Jena Coffey, Sunset Hills, MO*

PREP: 20 min. • **BAKE:** 25 min. • **MAKES:** 8 servings

1 can (10¾ oz.) condensed cream of mushroom soup, undiluted
1 cup whole milk
1 pkg. (6 oz.) stuffing mix
2 cups cubed cooked chicken breast
2 cups fresh broccoli florets, cooked
2 celery ribs, finely chopped
1½ cups shredded Swiss cheese, divided

1. Preheat oven to 375°. In a large bowl, combine soup and milk until blended. Add the stuffing mix with contents of seasoning packet, chicken, broccoli, celery and 1 cup cheese. Transfer to a greased 13x9-in. baking dish.

2. Bake, uncovered, for 20 minutes or until heated through. Sprinkle with the remaining cheese; bake 5 minutes longer or until the cheese is melted.

FREEZE OPTION: Sprinkle the remaining cheese over unbaked casserole. Cover and freeze. To use, partially thaw in refrigerator overnight. Remove from refrigerator 30 minutes before baking. Bake casserole as directed, increasing time as necessary to heat through and for a thermometer inserted in center to read 165°.

1 CUP: 247 cal., 7g fat (4g sat. fat), 42mg chol., 658mg sod., 24g carb. (0 sugars, 3g fiber), 22g pro.

SAUSAGE-STUFFED ACORN SQUASH

Acorn squash gets the sweet and savory treatment when stuffed with sausage, onion, spinach and cranberries. Cooking the squash in the microwave makes this quick enough for a busy weeknight.

—Taste of Home *Test Kitchen*

TAKES: 30 min. • **MAKES:** 4 servings

2   medium acorn squash
1   lb. bulk spicy pork sausage
½   cup chopped onion
1   cup fresh spinach, finely chopped
½   cup dried cranberries
1½ cups soft bread crumbs
1   large egg
2   Tbsp. 2% milk

1. Halve squash lengthwise; discard seeds. Place squash in a microwave-safe dish, cut side down. Microwave, covered, on high until tender, 10-12 minutes.

2. Meanwhile, in a large skillet, cook and crumble sausage with onion over medium heat until sausage is no longer pink, 5-7 minutes; drain. Remove from heat; stir in spinach, cranberries and bread crumbs. In a small bowl, whisk together egg and milk; add to the sausage mixture and toss until moistened.

3. Turn over squash; fill with the sausage mixture. Microwave, covered, until a thermometer inserted in the stuffing reads 165°, 2-3 minutes.

1 STUFFED SQUASH HALF: 485 cal., 23g fat (8g sat. fat), 133mg chol., 843mg sod., 49g carb. (18g sugars, 5g fiber), 25g pro.

✱ DID YOU KNOW?

To make soft bread crumbs, tear bread into pieces and place in a food processor or blender. Cover and pulse until crumbs form. One slice of bread yields ½-¾ cup crumbs.

CHICKEN CORDON BLEU BAKE

A friend shared this awesome hot dish with me. I make and freeze several pans at a time to share with neighbors or for days when I'm scrambling at mealtime.
—*Rea Newell, Decatur, IL*

PREP: 20 min. • **BAKE:** 40 min. • **MAKES:** 2 casseroles (6 servings each)

2 pkg. (6 oz. each) reduced-sodium stuffing mix
1 can (10¾ oz.) condensed cream of chicken soup, undiluted
1 cup 2% milk
8 cups cubed cooked chicken
½ tsp. pepper
¾ lb. sliced deli ham, cut into 1-in. strips
1 cup shredded Swiss cheese
3 cups shredded cheddar cheese

1. Preheat oven to 350°. Prepare stuffing mixes according to package directions. Meanwhile, whisk together soup and milk.

2. Toss chicken with pepper; divide between 2 greased 13x9-in. baking dishes. Layer with ham, Swiss cheese, 1 cup cheddar cheese, soup mixture and stuffing. Sprinkle with remaining cheddar cheese.

3. Bake, covered, for 30 minutes. Uncover; bake until the cheese is melted, 10-15 minutes.

FREEZE OPTION: Cover and freeze unbaked casseroles. To use, partially thaw in refrigerator overnight. Remove from refrigerator 30 minutes before baking. Preheat oven to 350°. Bake, covered, until heated through and a thermometer inserted in center reads 165°, about 45 minutes. Uncover; bake until cheese is melted, 10-15 minutes.

1 CUP: 555 cal., 29g fat (15g sat. fat), 158mg chol., 1055mg sod., 26g carb. (5g sugars, 1g fiber), 46g pro.

BEEF & BULGUR-STUFFED ZUCCHINI BOATS

My mom frequently cooked giant zucchini that she grew in her garden.
I adapted this recipe from one of her favorite weeknight meals.
Though I love the taste of fresh-picked zucchini, the ones
I've bought at the grocery store cook up fine, too.

—*Susan Peterson, Blaine, MN*

PREP: 35 min. • **BAKE:** 30 min. • **MAKES:** 4 servings

4   medium zucchini
1   lb. lean ground beef
    (90% lean)
1   large onion,
    finely chopped
1   small sweet red
    pepper, chopped
1½ cups tomato sauce
½   cup bulgur
¼   tsp. pepper
½   cup salsa
½   cup shredded
    reduced-fat
    cheddar cheese

1. Preheat oven to 350°. Cut each zucchini lengthwise in half. Scoop out pulp, leaving a ¼-in. shell; chop the pulp.

2. In a large skillet, cook beef, onion and red pepper over medium heat for 6-8 minutes or until the meat is no longer pink, breaking into crumbles; drain. Stir in tomato sauce, bulgur, pepper and zucchini pulp. Bring to a boil. Reduce heat; simmer, uncovered, 12-15 minutes or until bulgur is tender. Stir in salsa. Spoon into zucchini shells.

3. Place in a 13x9-in. baking dish coated with cooking spray. Bake, covered, for 20 minutes. Sprinkle with cheese. Bake, uncovered, 10-15 minutes longer or until the zucchini is tender and the filling is heated through.

2 STUFFED ZUCCHINI HALVES: 361 cal., 13g fat (6g sat. fat), 81mg chol., 714mg sod., 31g carb. (9g sugars, 7g fiber), 32g pro. *Diabetic exchanges:* 4 lean meat, 2 vegetable, 1 starch.

CHICKEN & DUMPLING CASSEROLE

This savory casserole is one of my husband's favorites. He loves the fluffy dumplings with plenty of gravy poured over them. The basil adds just the right touch of flavor and makes the whole house smell so good while this dish cooks.

—*Sue Mackey, Jackson, WI*

PREP: 30 min. • **BAKE:** 40 min. • **MAKES:** 8 servings

½ cup chopped onion
½ cup chopped celery
¼ cup butter, cubed
2 garlic cloves, minced
½ cup all-purpose flour
2 tsp. sugar
1 tsp. salt
1 tsp. dried basil
½ tsp. pepper
4 cups chicken broth
1 pkg. (10 oz.) frozen
   green peas
4 cups cubed
   cooked chicken

DUMPLINGS
2 cups biscuit/baking mix
2 tsp. dried basil
⅔ cup 2% milk

1. Preheat oven to 350°. In a large saucepan, saute the onion and celery in butter until tender. Add garlic; cook 1 minute longer. Stir in flour, sugar, salt, basil and pepper until blended. Gradually add the broth; bring to a boil. Cook and stir 1 minute or until thickened; reduce heat. Add peas and cook 5 minutes, stirring constantly. Stir in chicken. Pour into a greased 13x9-in. baking dish.

2. For the dumplings, in a small bowl, combine baking mix and basil. Stir in milk with a fork until moistened. Drop by tablespoonfuls into mounds over the chicken mixture.

3. Bake, uncovered, for 30 minutes. Cover and bake 10 minutes longer or until a toothpick inserted in a dumpling comes out clean.

1 SERVING: 393 cal., 17g fat (7g sat. fat), 80mg chol., 1313mg sod., 33g carb. (6g sugars, 3g fiber), 27g pro.

BEEF & TATER BAKE

The classic combination of beef and potatoes is extra convenient in this heartwarming, all-in-one dinner the whole family will enjoy.
—*Mike Tchou, Pepper Pike, OH*

PREP: 10 min. • **BAKE:** 35 min. • **MAKES:** 8 servings

4   cups frozen Tater Tots
1   lb. ground beef
¼   tsp. garlic powder
⅛   tsp. pepper
1   can (10¾ oz.) condensed cream of broccoli soup, undiluted
⅓   cup 2% milk
1   pkg. (16 oz.) frozen chopped broccoli, thawed
1   can (2.8 oz.) french-fried onions, divided
1   cup shredded Colby-Monterey Jack cheese, divided
1   medium tomato, chopped

1. Preheat oven to 400°. Spread Tater Tots evenly in an ungreased 13x9-in. baking dish. Bake, uncovered, for 10 minutes.

2. Meanwhile, in a large skillet, cook and crumble beef over medium heat until meat is no longer pink, 5-7 minutes; drain. Stir in the seasonings, soup, milk, broccoli, ¾ cup of onions, ½ cup of cheese and the tomato; heat through. Pour over potatoes.

3. Bake, covered, for 20 minutes. Sprinkle with the remaining onions and cheese. Bake, uncovered, until the cheese is melted, 5-10 minutes.

1 PIECE: 400 cal., 24g fat (9g sat. fat), 50mg chol., 805mg sod., 29g carb. (3g sugars, 4g fiber), 17g pro.

CORN, BEEF & TATER BAKE: Subsitute 1 package frozen corn for the broccoli and 1 can cream of celery soup for the cream of broccoli soup.

CORN DOG CASSEROLE

Reminiscent of traditional corn dogs, this fun main dish really
hits the spot and is always a winner with the kids.
It tastes especially good right from the oven.
—*Marcy Suzanne Olipane, Belleville, IL*

PREP: 25 min. • **BAKE:** 30 min. • **MAKES:** 10 servings

2 cups thinly sliced celery
2 Tbsp. butter
1½ cups sliced green onions
1½ lbs. hot dogs
2 large eggs
1½ cups 2% milk
2 tsp. rubbed sage
¼ tsp. pepper
2 pkg. (8½ oz. each)
  cornbread/muffin mix
2 cups shredded sharp
  cheddar cheese, divided

1. In a small skillet, saute celery in butter for 5 minutes. Add onions; saute 5 minutes longer or until vegetables are tender. Place in a large bowl; set aside.

2. Preheat oven to 400°. Cut hot dogs into ½-in. slices. In the same skillet, saute the hot dog slices until lightly browned, about 5 minutes; add to the vegetables.

3. In a large bowl, whisk eggs, milk, sage and pepper. Set aside 1 cup of the hot dog mixture; add the rest to the egg mixture. Stir in cornbread mixes. Add 1½ cups cheese. Spread into a shallow 3-qt. baking dish. Top with the reserved hot dog mixture and the remaining cheese.

4. Bake, uncovered, until golden brown, about 30 minutes.

1 CUP: 578 cal., 38g fat (16g sat. fat), 108mg chol., 1307mg sod., 40g carb. (13g sugars, 4g fiber), 19g pro.

CASHEW CHICKEN CASSEROLE

I especially like this tasty dish because I can get it ready the day before I need it. It's easy to whip up with common pantry items, including macaroni, canned soup and saltine crackers.
—*Julie Ridlon, Solway, MN*

PREP: 15 min. + chilling • **BAKE:** 35 min. • **MAKES:** 8 servings

2   cups uncooked elbow macaroni
3   cups cubed cooked chicken
½   cup process cheese (Velveeta)
1   small onion, chopped
½   cup chopped celery
½   cup chopped green pepper
1   can (8 oz.) sliced water chestnuts, drained
1   can (10¾ oz.) condensed cream of mushroom soup, undiluted
1   can (10¾ oz.) condensed cream of chicken soup, undiluted
1⅓ cups milk
1   can (14½ oz.) chicken broth
¼   cup butter, melted
⅔   cup crushed saltines (about 20 crackers)
¾   cup cashew halves

1. In a greased 13x9-in. baking dish, layer the first 7 ingredients in the order listed. In a large bowl, combine the soups, milk and broth. Pour over the casserole. Cover and refrigerate overnight.

2. Preheat oven to 350°. Toss the butter and cracker crumbs; sprinkle over the casserole. Top with cashews. Bake, uncovered, for 35-40 minutes or until macaroni is tender.

1¼ CUPS: 464 cal., 25g fat (9g sat. fat), 79mg chol., 1095mg sod., 36g carb. (6g sugars, 4g fiber), 24g pro.

BROCCOLI BEEF SUPPER

Broccoli is one of my favorite vegetables, so I'm constantly on the lookout for new ways to prepare it. This casserole gives you your meat, potatoes and vegetables all in one delicious dish!
—*Connie Bolton, San Antonio, TX*

PREP: 15 min. • **BAKE:** 35 min. • **MAKES:** 8 servings

4 cups frozen cottage fries
1 lb. ground beef
3 cups frozen chopped broccoli, thawed
1 can (2.8 oz.) french-fried onions, divided
1 medium tomato, chopped
1 can (10¾ oz.) condensed cream of celery soup, undiluted
1 cup shredded cheddar cheese, divided
½ cup whole milk
¼ tsp. garlic powder
¼ tsp. pepper

1. Preheat oven to 400°. Line bottom and sides of a greased 13x9-in. baking dish with cottage fries. Bake, uncovered, for 10 minutes.

2. Meanwhile, in a large skillet, cook the beef over medium heat until no longer pink; drain. Layer the beef, broccoli, half the onions and the tomato over the fries. In a small bowl, combine the soup, ½ cup cheese, the milk, garlic powder and pepper; pour over top.

3. Cover and bake at 400° for 20 minutes. Uncover; sprinkle with the remaining cheese and onions. Bake 2 minutes longer or until the cheese is melted.

1 CUP: 420 cal., 22g fat (9g sat. fat), 46mg chol., 529mg sod., 40g carb. (3g sugars, 3g fiber), 18g pro.

BAKED NECTARINE CHICKEN SALAD

My nectarine chicken casserole is a fun twist on a classic. Folks love the crunchy chow mein noodles on top. I love that I can make it a day in advance! It's great served with hot bread or rolls.

—*Faye Robinson, Pensacola, FL*

PREP: 15 min. • **BAKE:** 20 min. • **MAKES:** 8 servings

1⅓ cups mayonnaise
½ cup shredded
   Parmesan cheese
2 Tbsp. lemon juice
1 tsp. salt
1 tsp. onion powder
4 cups cubed
   cooked chicken
8 celery ribs, thinly sliced
4 medium nectarines,
   coarsely chopped
8 green onions, sliced
2 cans (3 oz. each) crispy
   chow mein noodles

1. Preheat oven to 375°. In a small bowl, mix the first 5 ingredients. In a large bowl, combine chicken, celery, nectarines and onions. Add the mayonnaise mixture; toss gently to coat.

2. Transfer to a greased 13x9-in. baking dish. Sprinkle with noodles. Bake, uncovered, until heated through, 20-25 minutes.

TO MAKE AHEAD: This can be made a day in advance. Cover and refrigerate the unbaked casserole. Remove from the refrigerator 30 minutes before baking. Sprinkle with noodles and bake as directed.

1¼ CUPS: 539 cal., 37g fat (7g sat. fat), 69mg chol., 911mg sod., 26g carb. (8g sugars, 3g fiber), 25g pro.

SWEET POTATO ENCHILADA STACK

Like an enchilada crossed with lasagna, this awesome stacked casserole
is loaded with black beans, sweet potato and tons of Mexican flavors.
—Taste of Home *Test Kitchen*

PREP: 20 min. • **BAKE:** 20 min. • **MAKES:** 6 servings

1   large sweet potato,
       peeled and cut
       into ½-in. cubes
1   Tbsp. water
1   lb. ground beef
1   medium onion,
       chopped
1   can (15 oz.) black
       beans, rinsed
       and drained
1   can (10 oz.)
       enchilada sauce
2   tsp. chili powder
½   tsp. dried oregano
½   tsp. ground cumin
3   flour tortillas (8 in.)
2   cups shredded
       cheddar cheese

1. Preheat oven to 400°. In a large microwave-safe bowl, combine sweet potato and water. Cover and microwave on high for 4-5 minutes or until potato is almost tender.

2. Meanwhile, in a large skillet, cook beef and onion over medium heat until meat is no longer pink; drain. Stir in beans, enchilada sauce, chili powder, oregano, cumin and sweet potato; heat through.

3. Place a flour tortilla in a greased 9-in. deep-dish pie plate; layer with a third each of the beef mixture and the cheese. Repeat the layers twice. Bake for 20-25 minutes or until bubbly.

1 PIECE: 457 cal., 22g fat (12g sat. fat), 87mg chol., 804mg sod., 39g carb. (6g sugars, 6g fiber), 29g pro.

HAM & VEGGIE CASSEROLE

I've paired ham with broccoli and cauliflower for years—it's a simple and classic flavor combination that my family loves. To complete this casserole dinner, I pass around homemade dinner rolls.

—*Sherri Melotik, Oak Creek, WI*

TAKES: 30 min. • **MAKES:** 4 servings

1 pkg. (16 oz.) frozen broccoli florets
1 pkg. (16 oz.) frozen cauliflower
2 tsp. plus 2 Tbsp. butter, divided
¼ cup seasoned bread crumbs
2 Tbsp. all-purpose flour
1½ cups 2% milk
¾ cup shredded sharp cheddar cheese
½ cup grated Parmesan cheese
1½ cups cubed fully cooked ham (about 8 oz.)
¼ tsp. pepper

1. Preheat oven to 425°. Cook broccoli and cauliflower according to the package directions; drain.

2. Meanwhile, in a small skillet, melt 2 tsp. butter. Add the bread crumbs; cook and stir over medium heat for 2-3 minutes or until lightly toasted. Remove from heat.

3. In a large saucepan, melt the remaining butter over medium heat. Stir in flour until smooth; gradually whisk in milk. Bring to a boil, stirring constantly; cook and stir 1-2 minutes or until thickened. Remove from heat; stir in cheeses until blended. Stir in ham, pepper and vegetables.

4. Transfer to a greased 8-in. square baking dish. Sprinkle with toasted crumbs. Bake, uncovered, until heated through, 10-15 minutes.

1½ CUPS: 420 cal., 23g fat (13g sat. fat), 89mg chol., 1233mg sod., 25g carb. (10g sugars, 6g fiber), 28g pro.

TURKEY & SPINACH STUFFING CASSEROLE

Dried cranberries may seem to be an odd ingredient for this dish,
but they add just a hint of sweetness that makes a simple casserole special.
And everyone knows how well turkey, stuffing and cranberries go together!
—*Gilda Lester, Millsboro, DE*

TAKES: 25 min. • **MAKES:** 4 servings

1 can (14½ oz.) reduced-sodium chicken broth
3 Tbsp. butter
3 cups stuffing mix
3 cups cubed cooked turkey
2 cups fresh baby spinach
½ cup dried cranberries
¾ cup shredded cheddar cheese

1. Preheat oven to 350°. In a large saucepan, bring broth and butter to a boil. Remove from heat. Add stuffing mix; stir until moistened. Stir in turkey, spinach and cranberries.

2. Transfer to a greased 11x7-in. baking dish. Sprinkle with cheese. Bake, uncovered, 10-15 minutes or until cheese is melted.

1¼ CUPS: 565 cal., 24g fat (12g sat. fat), 125mg chol., 1259mg sod., 43g carb. (15g sugars, 2g fiber), 42g pro.

GRILLED ZUCCHINI & PESTO PIZZA, 230

PIZZAS & PASTAS

Fun and filling, pizzas and pastas are always popular options—especially when it comes to the kids!

Creamy Spinach & Rigatoni Bake 210
Cranberry, Brie & Turkey Pizza 213
Shrimp Tortellini Pasta Toss 214
Angel Hair Pasta with Sausage & Spinach. 217
Chicken Thai Pizza 218
One-Skillet Lasagna 221
Barbecue Chicken Pizza 222
Game-Night Nacho Pizza 225
Baked Spaghetti. 226
Three-Cheese Meatball Mostaccioli. 229
Grilled Zucchini & Pesto Pizza 230
Steak & Blue Cheese Pizza 233
Porcini Mac & Cheese 234
Creamy Turkey Tetrazzini 237
Rich Chicken Alfredo Pizza. 238
Tomato Baguette Pizza 241
One-Pot Bacon Cheeseburger Pasta 242
Sausage Spaghetti Spirals 245
Meatball Pizza 246
Bacon & Spinach Pizza 249
Chicken Broccoli Shells. 250
Turkey Spaghetti Casserole 253

CREAMY SPINACH & RIGATONI BAKE

Macaroni and cheese is one of the ultimate comfort foods, and this dish gives it an intriguing Florentine twist.

—*Tammy Rex, New Tripoli, PA*

PREP: 25 min. • **BAKE:** 20 min. • **MAKES:** 10 servings

1 pkg. (16 oz.) rigatoni
8 oz. sliced pancetta, chopped
¾ cup butter, cubed
½ cup chopped onion
¾ cup all-purpose flour
1½ tsp. salt
¾ tsp. pepper
5¼ cups 2% milk
4 cups shredded Italian cheese blend
1 can (14 oz.) water-packed artichoke hearts, rinsed, drained and chopped
1 pkg. (10 oz.) frozen chopped spinach, thawed and squeezed dry
¼ cup shredded Parmesan cheese

1. Preheat oven to 375°. Cook rigatoni according to the package directions.

2. Meanwhile, in a large skillet, cook pancetta over medium heat until crisp, stirring occasionally. Remove with a slotted spoon; drain on paper towels. Discard drippings; wipe the skillet clean.

3. In the same pan, heat butter over medium-high heat. Add onion; cook and stir until tender. Stir in flour, salt and pepper until blended; gradually whisk in milk. Bring to a boil, stirring constantly; cook and stir until thickened, 2-3 minutes. Remove from heat. Stir in cheese blend until melted.

4. Stir in artichokes, spinach and pancetta. Drain rigatoni; add to the cheese sauce. Transfer to a greased 13x9-in. baking dish; sprinkle with Parmesan cheese.

5. Bake, uncovered, until golden brown and bubbly, 20-25 minutes.

1¼ CUPS: 643 cal., 35g fat (20g sat. fat), 99mg chol., 1438mg sod., 53g carb. (8g sugars, 3g fiber), 28g pro.

CRANBERRY, BRIE & TURKEY PIZZA

While traveling in New Zealand, my husband and I discovered turkey pizza.
We came up with our own version for a creative way to use leftovers.
—*Kristin Stone, Little Elm, TX*

TAKES: 25 min. • **MAKES:** 6 servings

1 prebaked 12-in. pizza crust
1 cup whole-berry cranberry sauce
1 tsp. grated orange zest
2 cups shredded part-skim mozzarella cheese
1 cup coarsely shredded cooked turkey
½ small red onion, thinly sliced
4 oz. Brie cheese, cubed
1 Tbsp. minced fresh rosemary

1. Preheat oven to 450°. Place pizza crust on an ungreased baking sheet.

2. In a small bowl, mix cranberry sauce and orange zest; spread over the crust. Top with mozzarella cheese, turkey, onion and Brie cheese; sprinkle with rosemary. Bake for 10-12 minutes or until the cheese is melted.

1 SLICE: 456 cal., 17g fat (9g sat. fat), 67mg chol., 768mg sod., 49g carb. (14g sugars, 2g fiber), 27g pro.

SHRIMP TORTELLINI PASTA TOSS

No matter how you toss 'em up, shrimp and thyme
play nicely with any spring-fresh vegetable.
—Taste of Home *Test Kitchen*

TAKES: 20 min. • **MAKES:** 4 servings

1 pkg. (9 oz.) refrigerated cheese tortellini
1 cup frozen peas
3 Tbsp. olive oil, divided
1 lb. uncooked shrimp (31-40 per lb.), peeled and deveined
2 garlic cloves, minced
¼ tsp. salt
¼ tsp. dried thyme
¼ tsp. pepper

1. Cook tortellini according to package directions, adding peas during the last 5 minutes of cooking.

2. Meanwhile, in a large nonstick skillet, heat 2 Tbsp. oil over medium-high heat. Add shrimp; cook and stir for 2 minutes. Add garlic; cook 1-2 minutes longer or until the shrimp turn pink.

3. Drain the tortellini; add to the skillet. Stir in salt, thyme, pepper and the remaining oil; toss to coat.

1¼ CUPS: 413 cal., 17g fat (4g sat. fat), 165mg chol., 559mg sod., 36g carb. (4g sugars, 3g fiber), 29g pro. *Diabetic exchanges:* 4 lean meat, 2 starch, 2 fat.

ANGEL HAIR PASTA WITH SAUSAGE & SPINACH

You won't miss the marinara sauce once you taste this
pasta dish flavored with chicken broth and Italian sausage.
My husband likes it so much that I make it once a week.
—*Daphine Smith, Baytown, TX*

TAKES: 30 min. • **MAKES:** 4 servings

4 Italian sausage links
(4 oz. each), sliced
1 medium onion,
chopped
2 garlic cloves, minced
2 tsp. olive oil
2 cans (14½ oz. each)
chicken broth
8 oz. uncooked angel hair
pasta, broken in half
2 pkg. (9 oz. each) fresh
spinach, trimmed and
coarsely chopped
2 Tbsp. all-purpose flour
¼ tsp. pepper
⅓ cup heavy
whipping cream

1. In a Dutch oven, cook the sausage, onion and garlic in oil over medium heat until the meat is no longer pink; drain. Add broth; bring to a boil. Add pasta; cook for 3 minutes, stirring frequently.

2. Gradually add spinach. Cook and stir for 2-3 minutes or until the pasta is tender and the spinach is wilted. In a small bowl, combine the flour, pepper and cream until smooth; gradually stir into pasta mixture. Bring to a boil; cook and stir for 1-2 minutes or until thickened.

1½ CUPS: 563 cal., 26g fat (10g sat. fat), 77mg chol., 1546mg sod., 57g carb. (6g sugars, 6g fiber), 25g pro.

CHICKEN THAI PIZZA

This is a recipe I make for my friends on a girl's night filled with fun and laughter. It is simple to make but is full of flavor.
—*Kimberly Knuppenburg, Menomonee Falls, WI*

TAKES: 25 min. • **MAKES:** 6 servings

1 prebaked 12-in. pizza crust
⅔ cup Thai peanut sauce
2 Tbsp. reduced-sodium soy sauce
2 Tbsp. creamy peanut butter
1 cup shredded cooked chicken breast
1 cup shredded part-skim mozzarella cheese
3 green onions, chopped
½ cup bean sprouts
½ cup shredded carrot

1. Preheat oven to 400°. Place unbaked crust on an ungreased 12-in. pizza pan or baking sheet. In a small bowl, combine peanut sauce, soy sauce and peanut butter. Add chicken; toss to coat. Spread mixture over crust; sprinkle with cheese and onions.

2. Bake for 10-12 minutes or until the cheese is melted. Top with bean sprouts and shredded carrot.

1 SLICE: 361 cal., 15g fat (4g sat. fat), 29mg chol., 1183mg sod., 35g carb. (4g sugars, 3g fiber), 23g pro.

ONE-SKILLET LASAGNA

This is hands-down one of the best skillet lasagna recipes we've ever tasted. With classic flavors and cheesy layers, it's definitely kid-friendly.
—Taste of Home *Test Kitchen*

TAKES: 30 min. • **MAKES:** 6 servings

¾ lb. ground beef
2 garlic cloves, minced
1 can (14½ oz.) diced tomatoes with basil, oregano and garlic, undrained
2 jars (14 oz. each) spaghetti sauce
⅔ cup condensed cream of onion soup, undiluted
2 large eggs, lightly beaten
1¼ cups 1% cottage cheese
¾ tsp. Italian seasoning
9 no-cook lasagna noodles
½ cup shredded Colby-Monterey Jack cheese
½ cup shredded part-skim mozzarella cheese

1. In a large skillet, cook beef and garlic over medium heat until the meat is no longer pink; drain. Stir in tomatoes and spaghetti sauce; heat through. Transfer to a large bowl.

2. In a small bowl, combine the soup, eggs, cottage cheese and Italian seasoning.

3. Return 1 cup meat sauce to the skillet; spread evenly. Layer with 1 cup cottage cheese mixture, 1½ cups meat sauce and half the lasagna noodles, breaking to fit. Repeat layers of cottage cheese mixture, meat sauce and noodles. Top with the remaining meat sauce. Bring to a boil. Reduce heat; cover and simmer for 15-17 minutes or until noodles are tender.

4. Remove from the heat. Sprinkle with shredded cheeses; cover and let stand for 2 minutes or until cheese is melted.

1 SERVING: 478 cal., 20g fat (8g sat. fat), 128mg chol., 1552mg sod., 43g carb. (15g sugars, 4g fiber), 31g pro.

BARBECUE CHICKEN PIZZA

My husband and I love barbecue chicken pizza, but I took it up a notch by adding other toppings that we love, including smoky bacon and creamy Gorgonzola. My mouth starts to water just thinking about it!

—*Megan Crow, Lincoln, NE*

PREP: 30 min. • **BAKE:** 15 min. • **MAKES:** 8 servings

2 Tbsp. olive oil
1 medium red onion, sliced
1 tube (13.8 oz.) refrigerated pizza crust
¾ cup barbecue sauce
2 cups shredded cooked chicken breast
6 bacon strips, cooked and crumbled
¼ cup crumbled Gorgonzola cheese
2 jalapeno peppers, seeded and minced
1 tsp. paprika
1 tsp. garlic powder
2 cups shredded part-skim mozzarella cheese

1. Preheat oven to 425°. In a large skillet, heat olive oil over medium heat. Add onion; cook and stir 4-6 minutes or until softened. Reduce heat to medium-low; cook 20-25 minutes or until deep golden brown, stirring occasionally.

2. Unroll pizza crust and press onto bottom and ½ in. up sides of a greased 15x10x1-in. baking pan. Bake 8 minutes.

3. Spread barbecue sauce over pizza crust; top with chicken, onion, bacon, Gorgonzola cheese and jalapenos. Sprinkle with paprika and garlic powder; top with mozzarella cheese. Bake until crust is golden and cheese is melted, 8-10 minutes.

FREEZE OPTION: Bake pizza crust as directed; cool. Top with ingredients as directed, and securely wrap and freeze unbaked pizza. To use, unwrap pizza; bake as directed, increasing time as necessary.

NOTE: Wear disposable gloves when cutting hot peppers; the oils can burn exposed skin. Avoid touching your face.

1 PIECE: 354 cal., 15g fat (5g sat. fat), 53mg chol., 851mg sod., 29g carb. (7g sugars, 2g fiber), 25g pro.

GAME-NIGHT NACHO PIZZA

Some like it hot with jalapenos; others like it cool with a dollop of sour cream.
But one thing's for sure—this is "nacho" ordinary pizza night!
—*Jamie Jones, Madison, GA*

....

TAKES: 20 min. • **MAKES:** 6 servings

1 **prebaked 12-in. pizza crust**
1 **Tbsp. olive oil**
1 **cup refried beans**
1 **cup refrigerated fully cooked barbecued shredded beef**
½ **cup chopped seeded tomatoes**
½ **cup pickled jalapeno slices**
1 **cup shredded Colby-Monterey Jack cheese**
   Optional toppings: shredded lettuce, sour cream and salsa

1. Preheat oven to 450°. Place crust on an ungreased pizza pan. Brush with oil. Spread beans over crust. Top with beef, tomatoes, jalapenos and cheese.

2. Bake until the cheese is melted, 10-15 minutes. Serve with lettuce, sour cream and salsa if desired.

1 SERVING: 370 cal., 13g fat (5g sat. fat), 30mg chol., 1103mg sod., 46g carb. (6g sugars, 3g fiber), 18g pro.

BAKED SPAGHETTI

This cheesy delight puts a different spin on spaghetti. Leftovers—
if there are any—freeze well for a quick future meal.
—*Ruth Koberna, Brecksville, OH*

PREP: 30 min. • **BAKE:** 30 min. • **MAKES:** 12 servings

1 cup chopped onion
1 cup chopped green pepper
1 Tbsp. butter
1 can (28 oz.) diced tomatoes, undrained
1 can (4 oz.) mushroom stems and pieces, drained
1 can (2¼ oz.) sliced ripe olives, drained
2 tsp. dried oregano
1 lb. ground beef, browned and drained, optional
12 oz. spaghetti, cooked and drained
2 cups shredded cheddar cheese
1 can (10¾ oz.) condensed cream of mushroom soup, undiluted
¼ cup water
¼ cup grated Parmesan cheese

1. Preheat oven to 350°. In a large skillet, saute chopped onion and green pepper in butter until tender. Add tomatoes, mushrooms, olives, oregano and, if desired, ground beef. Simmer, uncovered, for 10 minutes.

2. Place half of the spaghetti in a greased 13x9-in. baking dish. Layer with half of the vegetable mixture and 1 cup cheddar cheese. Repeat the layers.

3. In a small bowl, combine soup and water until smooth; pour over the casserole. Sprinkle with Parmesan cheese. Bake, uncovered, until heated through, 30-35 minutes.

1 CUP: 239 cal., 9g fat (5g sat. fat), 25mg chol., 500mg sod., 30g carb. (5g sugars, 3g fiber), 10g pro.

✷ TEST KITCHEN TIP

To prevent pasta from sticking together when cooking, use a large pot and 3 qt. of water for each 8 oz. of pasta you plan to cook. Add 1 Tbsp. cooking oil to the water. (This also prevents boiling over.) Bring the water to a full rolling boil before stirring in the pasta. Stir several times to separate the pasta until the water returns to a boil.

THREE-CHEESE MEATBALL MOSTACCIOLI

When my husband travels for work, I make a special dinner for my kids to keep their minds off missing Daddy. This tasty mostaccioli is meatball magic.
—*Jennifer Gilbert, Brighton, MI*

PREP: 15 min. • **BAKE:** 35 min. • **MAKES:** 10 servings

1 pkg. (16 oz.) mostaccioli
2 large eggs,
   lightly beaten
1 carton (15 oz.) part-skim
   ricotta cheese
1 lb. ground beef
1 medium onion,
   chopped
1 Tbsp. brown sugar
1 Tbsp. Italian seasoning
1 tsp. garlic powder
¼ tsp. pepper
2 jars (24 oz. each) pasta
   sauce with meat
½ cup grated
   Romano cheese
1 pkg. (12 oz.) frozen
   fully cooked Italian
   meatballs, thawed
¾ cup shaved
   Parmesan cheese
   Minced fresh parsley
   or fresh baby arugula,
   optional

1. Preheat oven to 350°. Cook mostaccioli according to package directions for al dente; drain. Meanwhile, in a small bowl, mix eggs and ricotta cheese.

2. In a 6-qt. stockpot, cook the beef and onion for 6-8 minutes or until beef is no longer pink, breaking up meat into crumbles; drain. Stir in brown sugar and seasonings. Add the pasta sauce and mostaccioli; toss to combine.

3. Transfer half of the pasta mixture to a greased 13x9-in. baking dish. Layer with ricotta mixture and remaining pasta mixture; sprinkle with Romano cheese. Top with meatballs and Parmesan cheese.

4. Bake, uncovered, 35-40 minutes or until heated through. If desired, top with parsley.

1⅓ CUPS: 541 cal., 23g fat (11g sat. fat), 105mg chol., 1335mg sod., 55g carb. (13g sugars, 5g fiber), 34g pro.

GRILLED ZUCCHINI & PESTO PIZZA

In the great outdoors, we surprise fellow campers who don't think it's possible to have standout pizza in the backwoods. This one with zucchini proves our point!
—*Jesse Arriaga, Reno, NV*

TAKES: 20 min. • **MAKES:** 6 servings

4 naan flatbreads
½ cup prepared pesto
2 cups shredded part-skim mozzarella cheese
1 medium zucchini, thinly sliced
1 small red onion, thinly sliced
¼ lb. thinly sliced hard salami, chopped
½ cup fresh basil leaves, thinly sliced
¼ cup grated Romano cheese

1. Over each naan, spread 2 Tbsp. pesto; top with ½ cup mozzarella and one-fourth of zucchini, onion and salami.

2. Grill, covered, over medium-low heat until the mozzarella has melted and the vegetables are tender, 4-6 minutes. Rotate naan halfway through grilling for an evenly browned crust.

3. Remove from heat. Top each naan with basil and Romano; cut into thirds.

2 PIECES : 391 cal., 24g fat (9g sat. fat), 51mg chol., 1276mg sod., 25g carb. (4g sugars, 1g fiber), 20g pro.

STEAK & BLUE CHEESE PIZZA

With sirloin steak and blue cheese, this is an unexpectedly elegant pizza. When I have a little extra time to play, I caramelize the onion to add a different flavor.
—*Kadija Bridgewater, Boca Raton, FL*

TAKES: 30 min. • **MAKES:** 6 servings

½ lb. beef top sirloin steak, thinly sliced
¼ tsp. salt
¼ tsp. pepper
2 Tbsp. olive oil, divided
2 cups sliced baby portobello mushrooms
1 large onion, sliced
½ cup heavy whipping cream
¼ cup crumbled blue cheese
1 prebaked 12-in. pizza crust
2 tsp. minced fresh parsley

1. Preheat oven to 450°. Sprinkle beef with salt and pepper. In a large skillet, heat 1 Tbsp. oil over medium heat. Add beef and mushrooms; cook for 3-4 minutes or until the beef is no longer pink. Remove from pan.

2. Cook onion in the remaining oil for 2-3 minutes or until tender. Add cream and blue cheese; cook 3-5 minutes longer or until slightly thickened.

3. Place crust on a 12-in. pizza pan or baking sheet. Spread with the cream mixture; top with the beef mixture. Sprinkle with parsley. Bake 10-12 minutes or until sauce is bubbly and crust is lightly browned.

1 SLICE: 365 cal., 19g fat (8g sat. fat), 47mg chol., 535mg sod., 33g carb. (3g sugars, 2g fiber), 18g pro.

PORCINI MAC & CHEESE

This recipe was inspired by the mac and cheese at a local restaurant. I added the fall flavor of a pumpkin ale, and it turned out even better than the original!
—*Laura Davis, Chincoteague, VA*

PREP: 30 min. + standing • **BAKE:** 35 min. • **MAKES:** 6 servings

1 pkg. (1 oz.) dried porcini mushrooms
1 cup boiling water
1 pkg. (16 oz.) small pasta shells
6 Tbsp. butter, cubed
1 cup chopped baby portobello mushrooms
1 shallot, finely chopped
1 garlic clove, minced
3 Tbsp. all-purpose flour
2½ cups 2% milk
½ cup pumpkin or amber ale
2 cups shredded sharp white cheddar cheese
1 cup shredded fontina cheese
1 tsp. salt
1 cup soft bread crumbs

1. Preheat oven to 350°. In a small bowl, combine the dried mushrooms and boiling water; let stand 15-20 minutes or until the mushrooms are softened. Remove with a slotted spoon; rinse and finely chop. Discard the liquid. Cook pasta according to package directions for al dente.

2. Meanwhile, in a Dutch oven, heat butter over medium-high heat. Add the portobello mushrooms and shallot; cook and stir 2-3 minutes or until tender. Add garlic; cook 1 minute longer. Stir in flour until blended; gradually stir in milk and beer. Bring to a boil, stirring constantly; cook and stir for 3-4 minutes or until slightly thickened. Stir in the cheeses, salt and reserved mushrooms.

3. Drain the pasta; add to the mushroom mixture and toss to combine. Transfer to a greased 13x9-in. baking dish. Top with bread crumbs. Bake, uncovered, for 35-40 minutes or until golden brown.

NOTE: To make soft bread crumbs, tear bread into pieces and place in a food processor or blender. Cover and pulse until crumbs form. One slice of bread yields ½-¾ cup crumbs.

1½ CUPS: 723 cal., 33g fat (19g sat. fat), 97mg chol., 968mg sod., 74g carb. (9g sugars, 4g fiber), 30g pro.

CREAMY TURKEY TETRAZZINI

What a great way to use up leftover turkey! This casserole bakes up delicious and bubbly for a wonderful main course.
—*Audrey Thibodeau, Gilbert, AZ*

PREP: 25 min. • **BAKE:** 50 min. • **MAKES:** 8 servings

1   pkg. (1 lb.) linguine
6   Tbsp. butter
6   Tbsp. all-purpose flour
½   tsp. salt
¼   tsp. pepper
⅛   tsp. cayenne pepper
3   cups chicken broth
1   cup heavy
    whipping cream
4   cups cubed
    cooked turkey
1   cup sliced fresh
    mushrooms
1   jar (4 oz.) diced
    pimientos, drained
¼   cup chopped
    fresh parsley
4   to 5 drops hot
    pepper sauce
⅓   cup grated
    Parmesan cheese

1. Preheat oven to 350°. Cook pasta according to the package directions. In a large saucepan, melt butter over medium heat. Stir in the flour, salt, pepper and cayenne until smooth. Gradually add broth. Bring to a boil; cook and stir for 2 minutes or until thickened. Remove from the heat; stir in cream.

2. Drain the linguine; add 2 cups sauce and toss to coat. Transfer to a greased 13x9-in. baking dish. Make a well in the center of the pasta, making a space about 6x4 in.

3. To the remaining sauce, add the turkey, mushrooms, pimientos, parsley and pepper sauce; mix well. Pour into the center of the dish. Sprinkle with cheese.

4. Cover and bake for 30 minutes. Uncover; bake until bubbly and heated through, 20-30 minutes longer.

1 SERVING: 540 cal., 25g fat (14g sat. fat), 132mg chol., 729mg sod., 49g carb. (4g sugars, 3g fiber), 31g pro.

RICH CHICKEN ALFREDO PIZZA

After a busy day, settle in for this appetizing homemade pizza. With a prebaked crust and simple Alfredo sauce, it's easy and delicious.
—*Tammy Hanks, Gainsville, FL*

PREP: 30 min. • **BAKE:** 15 min. • **MAKES:** 1 pizza (8 main dish or 12 appetizer slices)

2½ tsp. butter
1 garlic clove, minced
1½ cups heavy whipping cream
3 Tbsp. grated Parmesan cheese
½ tsp. salt
¼ tsp. pepper
1 Tbsp. minced fresh parsley
1 prebaked 12-in. thin pizza crust
1 cup cubed cooked chicken breast
1 cup thinly sliced baby portobello mushrooms
1 cup fresh baby spinach
2 cups shredded part-skim mozzarella cheese

1. Preheat oven to 450°. In a small saucepan over medium heat, melt butter. Add garlic; cook and stir for 1 minute. Add cream; cook until liquid is reduced by half, 15-20 minutes. Add Parmesan cheese, salt and pepper; cook and stir until thickened. Remove from the heat; stir in parsley. Cool slightly.

2. Place the crust on an ungreased baking sheet; spread with the cream mixture. Top with chicken, mushrooms, spinach and mozzarella cheese. Bake for 15-20 minutes or until the cheese is melted and the crust is golden brown.

1 SLICE: 391 cal., 26g fat (15g sat. fat), 87mg chol., 612mg sod., 21g carb. (3g sugars, 1g fiber), 18g pro.

TOMATO BAGUETTE PIZZA

When my tomatoes ripen all at once, I use them up in simple recipes like this one. Cheesy baguette pizzas, served with a salad, are ideal for lunch—and they make standout appetizers, too.
—*Lorraine Caland, Shuniah, ON*

PREP: 25 min. • **BAKE:** 10 min. • **MAKES:** 6 servings

2 tsp. olive oil
8 oz. sliced fresh mushrooms
2 medium onions, halved and sliced
2 garlic cloves, minced
½ tsp. Italian seasoning
¼ tsp. salt
   Dash pepper
1 French bread baguette (10½ oz.), halved lengthwise
1½ cups shredded part-skim mozzarella cheese
¾ cup thinly sliced fresh basil leaves, divided
3 medium tomatoes, sliced

1. Preheat oven to 400°. In a large skillet, heat oil over medium-high heat; saute mushrooms and onions until tender. Add garlic and seasonings; cook and stir for 1 minute.

2. Place baguette halves on a baking sheet, cut side up; sprinkle with half the cheese and ½ cup basil. Top with the mushroom mixture, tomatoes and the remaining cheese.

3. Bake until the cheese is melted, 10-15 minutes. Sprinkle with the remaining basil. Cut each half into three portions.

1 PIECE: 260 cal., 7g fat (4g sat. fat), 18mg chol., 614mg sod., 36g carb. (5g sugars, 3g fiber), 13g pro. *Diabetic exchanges:* 2 starch, 1 vegetable, 1 medium-fat meat.

ONE-POT BACON CHEESEBURGER PASTA

When the weather's too chilly to grill burgers, I whip up a big pot of
this cheesy pasta. Believe it or not, it tastes just like a bacon cheeseburger,
and it's much easier for my young children to enjoy.
—*Carly Terrell, Granbury, TX*

TAKES: 15 min. • **MAKES:** 12 servings

8   bacon strips, chopped
2   pounds ground beef
½   large red onion, chopped
12 ounces uncooked spiral pasta
4   cups chicken broth
2   cans (15 oz. each) crushed tomatoes
1   can (8 oz.) tomato sauce
1   cup water
¼   cup ketchup
3   tablespoons prepared mustard
2   tablespoons Worcestershire sauce
¼   teaspoon salt
¼   teaspoon pepper
2   cups shredded cheddar cheese, divided
⅓   cup chopped dill pickle
    Optional toppings: Chopped tomatoes, shredded lettuce, sliced pickles and sliced red onion

1. In a 6-qt. stockpot, cook bacon over medium heat, stirring occasionally, until crisp, 6-8 minutes. Remove with a slotted spoon; drain on paper towels. Discard drippings.

2. In the same pot, cook ground beef and onion over medium heat, breaking into crumbles, until meat is no longer pink, 6-8 minutes; drain. Add the next 10 ingredients; bring to a boil. Reduce heat; simmer, covered, until pasta is al dente, stirring occasionally, about 10 minutes.

3. Stir in 1 cup of cheese, the pickle and bacon; cook and stir until the cheese is melted. Serve with the remaining cheese and, if desired, tomatoes, lettuce, pickles and red onions.

1⅓ CUPS: 390 cal., 18g fat (8g sat. fat), 73mg chol., 1023mg sod., 31g carb. (7g sugars, 3g fiber), 25g pro.

✱ TEST KITCHEN TIP

- Take the extra time and shred cheese from a block for this recipe; it will stir in with a smoother texture than pre-shredded cheese.
- This dish is great for kids; use Dijon mustard if you want a more "grown-up" taste.

SAUSAGE SPAGHETTI SPIRALS

My family loves this pasta casserole with hearty chunks of sausage and green pepper. The recipe makes a big pan, so it's nice for gatherings.
—*Carol Carolton, Wheaton, IL*

PREP: 15 min. • **BAKE:** 30 min. • **MAKES:** 6 servings

1 lb. bulk Italian sausage
1 medium green pepper, chopped
5 cups spiral pasta, cooked and drained
1 jar (24 oz.) spaghetti sauce
1½ cups shredded part-skim mozzarella cheese

1. Preheat oven to 350°. In a large skillet, cook the sausage and green pepper over medium heat until the meat is no longer pink; drain. Stir in pasta and spaghetti sauce.

2. Transfer to a greased 13x9-in. baking dish. Cover and bake for 25 minutes. Uncover; sprinkle with mozzarella cheese. Bake 5-10 minutes longer or until the cheese is melted.

1 SERVING: 592 cal., 24g fat (9g sat. fat), 59mg chol., 1071mg sod., 67g carb. (12g sugars, 5g fiber), 26g pro.

MEATBALL PIZZA

I always keep meatballs and pizza crusts in the freezer to make this specialty on the spur of the moment. Add a tossed salad, and you have a delicious dinner.
—*Mary Humeniuk-Smith, Perry Hall, MD*

TAKES: 25 min. • **MAKES:** 8 slices

1 prebaked 12-in. pizza crust
1 can (8 oz.) pizza sauce
1 tsp. garlic powder
1 tsp. Italian seasoning
¼ cup grated Parmesan cheese
1 small onion, halved and sliced
12 frozen fully cooked Italian meatballs (½ oz. each), thawed and halved
1 cup shredded part-skim mozzarella cheese
1 cup shredded cheddar cheese

1. Preheat oven to 350°. Place pizza crust on an ungreased 12-in. pizza pan or baking sheet.

2. Spread sauce over the crust; sprinkle with garlic powder, Italian seasoning and Parmesan cheese. Top with onion and meatballs; sprinkle with the remaining cheeses. Bake 12-17 minutes or until cheese is melted.

1 SLICE: 321 cal., 16g fat (8g sat. fat), 36mg chol., 755mg sod., 28g carb. (3g sugars, 2g fiber), 17g pro.

BACON & SPINACH PIZZA

Our go-to pizza is a snap to make using packaged pizza crust and ready-to-serve bacon. The kids don't even mind the spinach on top!
—*Annette Riva, Naperville, IL*

TAKES: 20 min. • **MAKES:** 6 servings

1 prebaked 12-in. pizza crust
⅓ cup pizza sauce
1 cup shaved Parmesan cheese
2 cups fresh baby spinach, thinly sliced
8 ready-to-serve fully cooked bacon strips, cut into 1-in. pieces

Preheat oven to 450°. Place pizza crust on an ungreased baking sheet. Spread with sauce; top with ½ cup cheese, spinach and bacon. Sprinkle with remaining cheese. Bake until the cheese is melted, 8-10 minutes.

1 SLICE: 269 cal., 10g fat (4g sat. fat), 10mg chol., 726mg sod., 31g carb. (2g sugars, 2g fiber), 15g pro. *Diabetic exchanges:* 2 starch, 2 medium-fat meat.

CHICKEN BROCCOLI SHELLS

This cheesy entree is a make-ahead dream. Just assemble it ahead of time and put it in the oven when company arrives. I round out the meal with a tossed salad and warm bread.
—*Karen Jagger, Columbia City, IN*

PREP: 15 min. • **BAKE:** 30 min. • **MAKES:** 7 servings

- 1 jar (16 oz.) Alfredo sauce
- 2 cups frozen chopped broccoli, thawed
- 2 cups diced cooked chicken
- 1 cup shredded cheddar cheese
- ¼ cup shredded Parmesan cheese
- 21 jumbo pasta shells, cooked and drained

Preheat oven to 350°. In a large bowl, combine the Alfredo sauce, broccoli, chicken and cheeses. Spoon mixture into pasta shells. Place in a greased 13x9-in. baking dish. Cover and bake for 30-35 minutes or until heated through.

FREEZE OPTION: Cover and freeze unbaked casserole. To use, partially thaw in refrigerator overnight. Remove from refrigerator 30 minutes before baking. Bake the casserole as directed, increasing time as necessary to heat through and for a thermometer inserted in center to read 165°.

3 SHELLS: 355 cal., 16g fat (9g sat. fat), 72mg chol., 453mg sod., 28g carb. (2g sugars, 2g fiber), 24g pro.

TURKEY SPAGHETTI CASSEROLE

My mom made this creamy spaghetti when I was growing up. Whenever I have any leftover chicken or turkey, I look forward to preparing this simple, tasty dinner.
—*Casandra Hetrick, Lindsey, OH*

PREP: 30 min. • **BAKE:** 1¼ hours • **MAKES:** 6 servings

1 medium onion, chopped
1 medium carrot, chopped
1 celery rib, chopped
⅓ cup sliced fresh mushrooms
1 Tbsp. butter
2½ cups reduced-sodium chicken broth
1 can (10¾ oz.) reduced-fat reduced-sodium condensed cream of mushroom soup, undiluted
¼ tsp. salt
¼ tsp. pepper
2½ cups cubed cooked turkey breast
6 oz. uncooked spaghetti, broken into 2-in. pieces
½ cup shredded reduced-fat Colby-Monterey Jack cheese
½ tsp. paprika

1. Preheat oven to 350°. In a small skillet, saute the onion, carrot, celery and mushrooms in butter until tender. In a large bowl, combine the broth, soup, salt and pepper.

2. In a 2½-qt. baking dish coated with cooking spray, layer the turkey, spaghetti and vegetable mixture. Pour broth mixture over the top.

3. Cover and bake for 70-80 minutes or until the spaghetti is tender, stirring once. Uncover; sprinkle with cheese and paprika. Bake 5-10 minutes longer or until the cheese is melted.

1 CUP: 284 cal., 6g fat (3g sat. fat), 62mg chol., 702mg sod., 30g carb. (4g sugars, 3g fiber), 26g pro. *Diabetic exchanges:* 3 lean meat, 1½ starch, 1 vegetable, ½ fat.

RECIPE INDEX

A

Angel Hair Pasta with
Sausage & Spinach...217
Apple Chicken Stew....129

B

Bacon & Spinach
Pizza 249
Baked Nectarine
Chicken Salad 200
Baked Spaghetti.......226
Balsamic Roasted
Chicken Thighs with
Root Vegetables......27
Barbecue Chicken
Pizza 222
Beef & Bulgur-Stuffed
Zucchini Boats.......188
Beef & Tater Bake 192
Black Bean &
Corn Quinoa 72
Blackened Tilapia with
Zucchini Noodles 51
Broccoli Beef Supper...199

C

Cacciatore Chicken
Breasts 71
Caesar Salmon with
Roasted Tomatoes
& Artichokes..........31
Carolina Shrimp &
Cheddar Grits........130
Cashew Chicken
Casserole............196
Cazuela 82
Chicken & Dumpling
Casserole............191
Chicken & Orzo
Skillet 48
Chicken & Swiss
Stuffing Bake........183
Chicken Broccoli
Shells................250
Chicken Burrito
Skillet 44
Chicken Chili with
Black Beans..........117
Chicken Cordon
Bleu Bake............187

Chicken Thai Pizza 218
Chicken Thighs
with Shallots
& Spinach 79
Chicken Veggie
Skillet 60
Cilantro Shrimp
& Rice 76
Cod & Asparagus
Bake 35
Corn Dog
Casserole............195
Cranberry, Brie
& Turkey Pizza 213
Cranberry Chicken
& Wild Rice 175
Cranberry Sweet
& Sour Pork...........63
Creamy Bratwurst
Stew 149
Creamy Spinach &
Rigatoni Bake 210
Creamy Turkey
Tetrazzini............237
Creole Jambalaya......118

Crescent Turkey
    Casserole 180
Curry-Roasted Turkey
    & Potatoes. 8

E

Easy Chicken
    & Dumplings 98

F

Favorite Hamburger
    Stew 105
Finnish Meat Pie 172
Fire-Roasted Ziti
    with Sausage 85

G

Game-Night
    Nacho Pizza 225
German Potato Salad
    with Sausage 158
Grilled Zucchini
    & Pesto Pizza 230

H

Ham & Veggie
    Casserole. 204
Hearty Brunswick
    Stew 94

I

Inside-Out Stuffed
    Cabbage 102

L

Lamb Stew 101
Lemon-Dijon Pork
    Sheet-Pan Supper 11
Lora's Pressure-Cooker
    Red Beans & Rice. 157

M

Mahi Mahi & Veggie
    Skillet 52
Manchester Stew 154
Mediterranean
    Spinach & Beans 67
Mediterranean
    Tilapia. 24
Meatball Pizza. 246
Mom's Paella 55

N

New England Lamb
    Bake 179
North African
    Chicken & Rice. 161

O

Oktoberfest Pork
    Roast. 141

One-Pot Spaghetti
    Dinner 97
One-Pot Bacon
    Cheeseburger
    Pasta 242
One-Skillet Lasagna. . . . 221
Orange-Glazed
    Pork with
    Sweet Potatoes. 36

P

Pan-Roasted Chicken
    & Vegetables 32
Parmesan Chicken with
    Artichoke Hearts. 16
Pasta & Broccoli
    Sausage Simmer. 89
Pierogi Beef Skillet 75
Porcini Mac & Cheese . . 234
Pork & Asparagus
    Sheet-Pan Dinner. 19
Pork & Green Chile
    Casserole. 168
Pressure-Cooker
    Buffalo Shrimp
    Mac & Cheese 126
Pressure-Cooker
    Chicken Tikka
    Masala 165
Pressure-Cooker
    Cuban Ropa Vieja. . . . 146
Pressure-Cooker
    Italian Shrimp &
    Pasta 153

Pressure-Cooker
    Mediterranean
    Chicken Orzo 133
Pressure-Cooker Sweet
    & Sour Pork 150
Pressure-Cooker
    Tuna Noodle
    Casserole 138

R
Reuben Bread
    Pudding 176
Rich Chicken Alfredo
    Pizza 238
Roasted Curried
    Chickpeas &
    Cauliflower 28

S
Sausage & Kale Lentil
    Stew 121
Sausage & Vegetable
    Skillet Dinner 43
Sausage Spaghetti
    Spirals 245
Sausage-Stuffed
    Acorn Squash 184
Savory Braised Chicken
    with Vegetables 106
Seafood Gumbo 90
Shrimp Risotto 47
Shrimp Tortellini
    Pasta Toss 214

Skillet BBQ Beef
    Potpie 68
Skillet Zucchini
    & Sausage 64
Slow-Cooked Beef
    & Veggies 137
Slow-Cooked
    Enchilada
    Casserole 142
Slow-Cooker
    Chicken Bog 145
Slow-Cooker Spicy
    Pork Chili 134
Slow-Simmered
    Burgundy
    Beef Stew 110
Spanish Rice with
    Chicken & Peas 86
Spicy Roasted
    Sausage, Potatoes
    & Peppers 20
Spinach & Chicken
    Phyllo Pie 171
Steak & Blue Cheese
    Pizza 233
Stout & Shiitake
    Pot Roast 93
Stovetop Tarragon
    Chicken 122
Sunday Cassoulet 114
Sweet & Tangy
    Salmon with
    Green Beans 12
Sweet Potato
    Enchilada Stack 203

T
Tasty Turkey Skillet 40
Three-Cheese
    Meatball
    Mostaccioli 229
Tomato Baguette
    Pizza 241
Tomato-Poached
    Halibut 59
Turkey & Spinach
    Stuffing Casserole . . . 207
Turkey Dumpling
    Stew 109
Turkey Lattice Pie 15
Turkey Spaghetti
    Casserole 253
Turkey-Stuffed
    Bell Peppers 23

V
Veg Jambalaya 113

W
Wasabi Beef Fajitas 56

Z
Zesty Beef Stew 162